Praise for Michael Gelb and *Creativity on Demand*

"There is only a thin veil separating our ordinary moments from great, creative achievements. In *Creativity on Demand,* Michael Gelb teaches us to part this veil and realize the potentials that are inherent in every one of us."

LARRY DOSSEY, MD, author of *One Mind:
How Our Individual Mind Is Part of a Greater Consciousness and Why It Matters*

"If you are in a leadership role it's more important than ever before for you to be creative and to bring out the creativity in your team. In this original and compelling book, Michael Gelb illuminates a simple, effective path for you to raise your baseline of creative energy and empower others to do the same."

JON MILLER, former CEO of AOL and chief digital officer of Newscorp

"Michael Gelb embodies the archetype of the Creative. Through his immensely popular seminars and writings he transmits state-of-the-art knowledge of the nature of genius, the working of the brain, and the quickening of creative energy. A master of the art of creative thinking, Michael will guide you in an exploration of your mind's potential that is uniquely entertaining and illuminating."

JEAN HOUSTON, PhD, author of *The Possible Human*

"*Creativity on Demand* is a treasure chest of concrete practices for bringing your inner spark out into the world—with heat, power, beauty, and grace."

ERICA ARIEL FOX, Harvard Law School lecturer and author of the *New York Times* bestseller *Winning from Within: A Breakthrough Method for Leading, Living, and Lasting Change*

"In a field cluttered with misinformation, Michael Gelb is an authentic source of practical wisdom for those who seek to develop their creative powers."

MURRAY GELL-MANN, Nobel Laureate in Physics

"Before your seminar, I thought that the world was divided into 'creative' people and the rest of us. As a reluctant former engineer and accidental marketing professor, I considered myself firmly in the latter camp—a terminally left-brain-dominated automaton to whom the world of inspired creativity would forever remain a mystery. You led me to a revelation. For the first time in my life, I realized that I had unique gifts to give, and that my life and work could rise above merely making a living to actually making a difference. Looking back, I mark this as the beginning of my own personal renaissance, a joyful journey of growth and self-discovery."

PROFESSOR RAJ SISODIA, author of *Firms of Endearment* and *Conscious Capitalism*

"Michael Gelb is a man of infinite energy, bursting creativity, and huge enthusiasm for life. He is a model, in short, of everything he celebrates and teaches."

TONY SCHWARTZ, author of *The Power of Full Engagement*

"Those who have watched Gelb in action know him as a master practitioner of many disciplines."
                                        TED HUGHES, former poet laureate of Great Britain

"*Creativity on Demand* is the result of a lifetime devoted to facilitating creativity in people and organizations. Whether your own interest is in cultivating the creative potential of other people or connecting more deeply with your personal talents and possibilities, it offers not only the inspiration, but also the practical guidance to help you make it happen."
                                        SIR KEN ROBINSON, PhD, from the Foreword

"Michael Gelb's brilliant book is filled with insight, inspiration, and enthusiasm. He has a refreshingly wide view, examining innovation from the perspective of ancient wisdom, and ancient wisdom from the vantage of 21st-century science. If you thought you knew what creativity was, or if you assumed that you were simply not one of the chosen few, think again. *Creativity on Demand* provides expert guidance in how to exercise creative energies so that you can better live your dreams. I recommend that you not only read this book, but also practice the mental and physical exercises within it. You will have the tools for greater success and fulfillment at work, and even more importantly, for greater health and happiness in everyday life!"
    KENNETH COHEN, author of *The Way of Qigong* and *The Essential Qigong Training Course*

"Michael Gelb is an astounding individual whose skills span a surprising and wide array of disciplines. All journeys of innovation must begin with—and include throughout—the skills and principles that he espouses. I can think of no one better qualified than him to advise us in this space."
                                        JIM KARKANIAS, senior director (partner) at Microsoft

"Do you want to know how to fill your cup with sparkling, juicy creative energy every day? Then read and rejoice—*Creativity on Demand* is a unique, practical, transformational resource for all who are passionate about living a great creative life!"
                                        SARK, author, artist, succulent wild woman

"Michael Gelb dives into each project he undertakes with full engagement and a high commitment to thorough excellence. His work on da Vinci and Edison are classics. In this volume, he has collected his own extensive experiences with aikido and qigong as well as the research of others into the dynamics of mind and body coordination. *Creativity on Demand* explains the theory and outlines multiple practical exercises designed to help readers experience the power that comes from coordinating mind and body. Thoughtful people in all professions will benefit from reading and following the wisdom expertly outlined here."
                                        JAMES G. CLAWSON,
    Johnson & Higgins Professor of Business, The Darden School, University of Virginia

"I really love the way this book is written. It is clear, simple, and very meaningful. The teachings are conveyed with remarkable precision and understanding. This work is wonderful!"   MASTER ROBERT PENG, author of *The Master Key*

"Are you hoping to make creativity a daily practice, but feel that what you're doing just isn't working? In his latest book, Michael Gelb shows us how to tap into a creative energy that's been recognized and cultivated for millennia. With examples drawn from a rich array of sources, both contemporary and ancient, this book might be the something different you've been looking for."

DANIEL H. PINK, author of *To Sell Is Human* and *Drive*

"This wonderful book is at once delightful, compelling, practical, funny, and informative. Reading it creates a feeling of excitement and possibility. Rich with helpful historical references, stories, and inspiration, you will also find detailed practical exercises that give you the 'how' of living more creatively and embodying your full potential."

WENDY PALMER, aikido sensei and author of *Leadership Embodiment*

"In *Creativity on Demand*, Michael Gelb offers surefire methods for cracking your individual creativity code, supplying your creative spirit wings upon which to soar. Truly, heaven's kiss of inspiration is firmly planted upon this book."

MICHAEL BERNARD BECKWITH, author of *Life Visioning*

"Michael Gelb does it again! *Creativity on Demand* pushes forward from where *How to Think Like Leonardo da Vinci* leaves off. He has ingenious—and creative!—ways of helping move you past your constraints. You will indeed become more creative if you practice the exercises he prescribes."

SRIKUMAR RAO, PhD, TED speaker
and author of *Happiness at Work: Be Resilient, Motivated, and Successful—No Matter What*

"I love Michael Gelb's unique perspective on qi. It's genius! This great book is a treasure chest of ancient wisdom made accessible for the modern world. As a teacher of qigong, Michael's charisma and creativity make traditional movements feel like exciting discoveries. His classes are engaging, inspiring, and fun."

LORIE DECHAR, senior clinical supervisor at the Tri-State College of Acupuncture
and author of *Five Spirits: Alchemical Acupuncture for Psychological and Spiritual Healing*

"Michael Gelb's ability to inspire creative thinking and esprit de corps is unparalleled. In this unique and extremely valuable book he explains how he does it, and how you can too."

GERRY KIRK, former managing director of Merck Sharp & Dohme Central America

"*Creativity on Demand* is a highly original mixture of inspiration and executive coaching that will help you claim the creativity that is your birthright. Michael J. Gelb has generated an outstanding wellspring for creative thinking and practical problem-solving—you'll find yourself reading it again and again to discover success and satisfaction in everything you do. And you'll be thrilled with the results!"

MARSHALL GOLDSMITH, top-ranked executive coach
and author of the global bestsellers *MOJO* and *What Got You Here Won't Get You There*

CREATIVITY

on

DEMAND

Also by Michael J. Gelb

Brain Power: Improve Your Mind as You Age
(with Kelly Howell, 2012)

Wine Drinking for Inspired Thinking:
Uncork Your Creative Juices (2010)

Innovate Like Edison: The Five-Step System for Breakthrough
Business Success (with Sarah Miller Caldicott, 2007)

Da Vinci Decoded: Discovering the Spiritual Secrets
of Leonardo's Seven Principles (2004)

More Balls Than Hands: Juggling Your Way to Success
by Learning to Love Your Mistakes (2003)

Discover Your Genius: How to Think Like History's
Ten Most Revolutionary Minds (2002)

The How to Think Like Leonardo da Vinci Workbook: Your Personal
Companion to How to Think Like Leonardo da Vinci (1999)

How to Think Like Leonardo da Vinci:
Seven Steps to Genius Every Day (1998)

Samurai Chess: Mastering Strategic Thinking Through
the Martial Art of the Mind (with Raymond Keene, 1997)

Thinking for a Change: Discovering the Power to Create,
Communicate, and Lead (1995)

Lessons from the Art of Juggling: How to Achieve Your Full Potential
in Business, Learning, and Life (with Tony Buzan, 1994)

Present Yourself!: Captivate Your Audience
with Great Presentation Skills (1988)

Body Learning: An Introduction to the Alexander Technique (1981)

CREATIVITY on DEMAND

How to Ignite and Sustain
the Fire of Genius

MICHAEL J. GELB

sounds true
BOULDER, COLORADO

Sounds True
Boulder, CO 80306

© 2014 Michael J. Gelb
Foreword © 2014 Ken Robinson
Photographs © 2014 Michael Myers

SOUNDS TRUE is a trademark of Sounds True, Inc.

This work is solely for personal growth and education. It should not be treated as a substitute
for professional assistance, therapeutic activities such as psychotherapy or counseling, or medical
advice. In the event of physical or mental distress, please consult with appropriate health
professionals. The application of protocols and information in this book is the choice of each
reader, who assumes full responsibility for his or her understandings, interpretations, and results.
The author and publisher assume no responsibility for the actions or choices of any reader.

Published 2014

Cover and book design by Jennifer Miles
Photographs by Michael Myers
Printed in the United States of America

For the Cataloging in Publication record (CIP data), please contact the publisher.

ISBN 978-1-62203-347-8
Ebook ISBN 978-1-62203-385-0
10 9 8 7 6 5 4 3 2 1

CONTENTS

CONTENTS

SIR KEN ROBINSON, PhD

How creative are you? How do you know? How can you discover and develop your real creative powers? These questions lie at the heart of this book, and Michael Gelb explores them with an assurance and compassion that come from a lifetime of expert practice and deep reflection.

There's enormous interest these days in creativity. Businesses everywhere, for example, know that their survival and their success depend on a constant flow of new ideas for products and services. Michael Gelb has worked for more than forty years with businesses of all sorts around the world. He has a lot to teach about how creativity works in organizations—about the obstacles to creativity and how to overcome them. Many of those lessons are contained in the pages that follow. But creativity is about more than business, and so is this book.

Properly conceived, creativity emerges from our most distinctive powers as human beings. Not much separates us from the rest of life on Earth, and we delude ourselves when we think it does. But in one respect, at least, we seem very different: we have powerful imaginations. By imagination, I mean the ability to bring into mind things that aren't present to our senses. In imagination we can visit the past, we can anticipate the future, and we can see beyond our immediate circumstances to other possible ways of being. Creativity grows from imagination, but it is a step beyond it. You could be imaginative all day long and never do anything. Creativity is the practical process of putting your imagination to work. Real creativity involves application, purpose, and a particular balance between freedom and control.

Our boundless capacities for creativity are evident in the breath-taking diversity of human achievements and cultures. In *Creativity on Demand*, Michael Gelb relates our powers of creativity to the traditional Chinese concept of *qi*, which translates roughly as "life force" or "vital energy." Other ancient cultures have comparable terms, such as *lung* in Tibetan Buddhism, the Hindu concept of *prana*, and *ruah* in Hebrew culture.

There is, of course, an important difference between potential and achievement. We may all have creative capacities, but not everyone realizes them. Down through the ages, teachers in many traditions have developed specific techniques to access and develop them. Michael Gelb has immersed himself in many of these practices, and the advice he gives here draws widely on them, with examples from many disciplines. Alongside time-honored practices of ancient cultures he sets out the findings of modern science. Often there are uncanny resonances between the two.

The most telling, everyday evidence of human creativity is that we all create our own lives, and we can re-create them too, if we have the will. It's for this reason that the book also has a lot to say, directly and indirectly, about attitude and mindset. It's why it begins with a series of questions to help you recognize and challenge the story you tell yourself about yourself.

Creativity on Demand is the result of a lifetime devoted to facilitating creativity in people and organizations. Whether your own interest is in cultivating the creative potential of other people or connecting more deeply with your own personal talents and possibilities, it offers not only the inspiration, but also the practical guidance to help you make it happen.

A Muse of Fire

O! for a muse of fire, that would ascend
the brightest heaven of invention.

William Shakespeare (1582-1616), Henry V[1]

What is creativity? Sir Ken Robinson, PhD, describes it as "the process of having original ideas that have value."[2] Betty Edwards, PhD, author of *Drawing on the Right Side of the Brain,* defines creativity as "the ability to find new solutions to a problem or new modes of expression."[3] And Wikipedia explains, "Creativity refers to the phenomenon whereby something new is created which has some kind of subjective value (such as an idea, a joke, a literary work, a painting or musical composition, a solution, an invention etc.). It is also the qualitative impetus behind any given act of creation."

Creativity has many forms and expressions. We may not be able to agree on a comprehensive definition, but like Supreme Court Justice Potter Stewart's observation on pornography, most of us "know it when we see it."

In our spam-infested world the ability to generate valuable, original ideas and to find new solutions is at a premium. It wasn't long ago that creativity was considered a luxury item. Today it is a necessity. Increasing complexity means that the demand for creativity in our personal and professional lives is greater than ever before.

This book is dedicated to helping you meet that demand.

Of course, for your original ideas to provide value they must be translated into action. Once you ignite the fire of genius it's essential to know how to sustain it. This book is dedicated to you if you want to know how to ignite and sustain your creative fire to empower every aspect of your life.

In *The Path of Least Resistance* Robert Fritz observed, "The most important developments in civilization have come through the creative process, but ironically, most people have not been taught to be creative."[4] This book is dedicated to ending that irony.

What kind of world would it be if we all learned how to be creative in the pursuit of our dreams? In *The War of Art* Steven Pressfield answers, "If tomorrow morning by some stroke of magic every dazed and benighted soul woke up with the power to take the first step towards pursuing his or her dreams, every shrink in the directory would be out of business. Prisons would stand empty. The alcohol and tobacco industries would collapse, along with the junk food, cosmetic surgery, and infotainment business, not to mention pharmaceutical companies, hospitals, and the medical profession from top to bottom. Domestic abuse would become extinct, as would addiction, obesity, migraine headaches, road rage, and dandruff."[5] This book is dedicated to the extinction of spiritual dandruff.

I'm dedicated to helping you discover and express your creative power.

When I was a child, the abominations of World War II, the tensions of the Cold War, and the injustices of racism and anti-semitism led me to think that there couldn't be a God or a meaning and purpose to life. I'd use my very active imagination to contemplate the vastness and emptiness of the universe, and this led me to experience gut-wrenching feelings of utter insignificance. At bedtime I'd squirm around, sweating under the sheets, often in a state of sheer terror.

Then in my early twenties, after intense practice of meditation and various spiritual disciplines, I realized that the universe was indeed vast and empty, but much to my surprise and delight, it was *an emptiness from which unlimited creative possibilities could manifest.* I read the words of a Chinese sage who describes this universal field of creativity as "the Great Mother, empty yet inexhaustible, it gives birth to infinite worlds." He adds, "It is always present within you, you can use it any way you want."[6]

In *Creativity on Demand* you'll learn how to access this infinite field and use it any way you want. For more than forty years I've explored how to help others apply this creative power. Then a few years ago I had another epiphahy, an "aha" experience, in which I realized the simplest, most profound way that we can all connect with the source of unlimited creative possibility. In that moment this book was born.

In the pages that follow you'll learn that the "fire of genius" is more than just a metaphor. Creative fire is a form of energy that is part of your birthright. But for many, the pilot light has gone out. You'll learn to ignite it and then how to cultivate and sustain it so that it grows more potent every day for the rest of your life.

RIDE THE WAVE

What-if questions are classic keys to unleashing creativity, so let's begin with a few:

- What if there is a source of creative energy that is inexhaustible, easily accessible, and free?
- What if the people we call geniuses, such as Leonardo da Vinci, Hildegard von Bingen, Nikola Tesla, and Marie Curie, had an intuitive understanding of how to connect with this source?
- What if for thousands of years people have been studying how to access, cultivate, store, and express creative energy?
- What if this wisdom, shrouded for millennia by esotericism and cultural prejudice, is now readily available?
- What if this book could teach you to apply that wisdom to raise your baseline of creative energy and insight?
- What if we combined this practical wisdom on accessing creative energy with an exploration of the most powerful methods for understanding and applying the creative process in your life now?

The answers are: There is. They did. They have been. It was and now it is. It will. And you will discover that you are more creative than you've ever imagined!

Creativity is my passion. I'm especially passionate about helping people develop and express their creativity. It's my profession, but it's also my life. Nothing gives me greater pleasure than helping someone realize his or her creative potential. Whether it's helping an aspiring author to write her first book, guiding a company to develop a more creative culture, or assisting a young friend in discovering his creative purpose, there's nothing that pleases me more. I do this by teaching tools for creative thinking and by a transmission of creative energy. That's what I want to do for you in this book.

Creativity: The Essential Twenty-First-Century Competency

In 1979 I co-directed my first five-day senior management retreat for the International Field Service Leadership Team of Digital Equipment Corporation (DEC). The theme was "utilizing creativity to deal with accelerating change." DEC's Field Service Leadership Team was ahead of the curve relative to the rest of the company. But their corporate leadership failed to anticipate the rise of the personal computer, and eventually Compaq acquired DEC.

Years later I gave a keynote speech at the global management conference for Compaq and reconnected with many of the participants from our original seminar. Then, a few years after that, I worked with Hewlett-Packard when it acquired Compaq. None of us knew, in that first seminar, just how fast change would accelerate.

The pace of change over the last forty years has led to all sorts of manuals on how to manage it. In 1998 Dr. Spencer Johnson published *Who Moved My Cheese?: An Amazing Way to Deal with Change in Your Work and in Your Life.* A parable with lovable mice as the protagonists, it has sold more than 30 million copies. The number one best-selling business book of all time illuminates readers with advice such as "change or face extinction" and "discover new cheese by giving up the old."[1] Johnson helped many people accept the rapid, unpredictable change that they faced in their professional and personal lives.

More recently, the Harvard Business School professor Deepak Malhotra released a book entitled *I Moved Your Cheese: For Those Who Refuse to Live as Mice in Someone Else's Maze.* Malhotra aims to show that rather than just accepting changing circumstances and reward systems, we can learn to think more creatively in order to change how we deal with our circumstances. As his protagonist Zed explains, "The problem is not that the mouse is in the maze, but the maze is in the mouse."[2] Malhotra emphasizes that independent creative thinking is the real key to success and fulfillment in our complex lives.

I agree. The zeitgeist (German for "spirit of the time"; *zeit* means "time," and *geist* means "spirit") has shifted toward the recognition that creativity is the most important "competency" for individuals and organizations. Evidence for this shift was offered in 2010 by IBM's Institute for Business Value survey of fifteen hundred chief executives, which aimed to ascertain the qualities that CEOs value in their people. Although "execution" and "engagement" continue to be highly valued, the CEOs had a new number-one priority: creativity.

For years creativity was seen as primarily the province of research and development, and marketing and advertising. It is only recently that organizations have realized that creativity is the key to successful leadership in an increasingly complex world. The IBM report concludes, "CEOs are signaling a new direction. They are telling us that a world of increasing complexity will give rise to a new generation of leaders that make creativity the path forward for successful enterprises." It adds, "Success requires fresh thinking and continuous innovation at all levels of the organization."[3]

Fresh thinking and continuous innovation are also necessary for anyone who wishes to lead a creative and fulfilling life. Fortunately, as you'll discover, contemporary neuroscience has overturned the old fixed-mindset paradigm that led many of us to believe that creativity couldn't be learned or developed. Now we know that we can continue improving our creative abilities throughout life.

Managing Energy: The Key to Creativity

Also in recent years, the best thinking on leadership and organizational performance has shifted away from the idea of managing time to recognize the importance of managing energy. One of the pioneers of this shift is James Clawson, the Johnson & Higgins Professor of Business Administration at the Darden Graduate School of Business at the University of Virginia. An innovator in the fields of leadership development and the relationship between energy/feel and performance, Clawson has consulted for executives at the highest levels in organizations including GE, Sallie Mae, Coca-Cola, USAA, British Aerospace USA, and Mass Mutual. I asked him to reflect on his forty years of experience in business and offer his most important insight about leadership.

He responded, "Leadership is about managing energy, first in yourself and then in those around you."[4]

When I asked him to elaborate, he explained, "Most executives want to know how to motivate others, when often the problem lies closer to home. When you walk into an organization, you can tell quickly what the energy level is—and therefore the quality of leadership in the place. If the energy level is low, the leadership is likely to be weak. If the energy level is high, there is likely to be good leadership in place."[5] In his book *Powered by Feel: How Individuals, Teams, and Companies Excel,* Clawson and his collaborator, Doug Newburg, observe that worldwide managers believe that how one feels affects performance, yet virtually none of them think about or focus on managing feel and/or energy. Clawson adds, "Energy management is the key to generating engagement, esprit de corps, and creative leadership."[6]

Jim Loehr and Tony Schwartz, authors of the *New York Times* bestseller *The Power of Full Engagement,* came to similar conclusions. They explain, "Leaders are stewards of organizational energy," and "[m]anaging energy, not time, is the key to enduring high performance as well as to health, happiness, and life balance." They emphasize:

- "Energy is the most important individual and organizational resource."

- "Every thought, feeling and action has an energy consequence."
- "Positive energy rituals—highly specific routines for managing energy—are the key to full engagement and sustained high performance."[7]

The sages of China came to these same conclusions five thousand years ago. Now we can apply this ancient wisdom to meeting the demand of our contemporary lives. In addition to learning and applying the creative mindset and methods of the creative process, the most important thing is to bring more geist to your zeit. Progress on the path of creative mastery comes as you learn to consciously cultivate your creative universal energy.

What Is Creative Universal Energy?

> At our most elemental, we are not a chemical reaction, but an energetic charge. Human beings and all living things are a coalescence of energy in a field of energy connected to every other thing in the world. This pulsating energy field is the central engine of our being and consciousness.
>
> Lynne McTaggart,
> The Field: The Quest for the Secret Force of the Universe[8]

All wisdom traditions acknowledge the existence of an infinite source of intelligent, creative energy in the universe. Let's refer to this creative universal energy with the acronym CUE (Creative Universal Energy). And, to make it simpler, we can represent that acronym with the letter Q. This energy has an intelligence of its own, so let's add an I to the abbreviation: QI, or qi. Pronounced "chee," qi just happens to be the Chinese word for intelligent, creative universal energy.

Quite interestingly, QI is also an acronym for "quality improvement," and there's no better way to improve the quality of your life than to learn how to access and play with qi.

Qi is the source of our vitality and creativity, and it connects us with all of creation. Mystics from many traditions have shared this understanding.

The Sufi poet Rumi (1207–1273) advises that you are a conduit for "the universe and the light of the stars."[9] The Hindu Vedas explain, "As is the microcosm so is the macrocosm. As is the atom so is the universe. As is the human body so is the cosmic body. As is the human mind so is the cosmic mind."[10] And the Chinese Taoist master Zhuangzi (369–286 BCE) observes, "The world and I have a common origin and all creatures and I together are one."[11]

This ancient wisdom is echoed in the observations of contemporary science. Physicist Carl Sagan (1934–1996) writes, "We are the local embodiment of a Cosmos grown to self-awareness."[12] Astrophysicist and director of the Hayden Planetarium Neil deGrasse Tyson elaborates, "Recognize that the very molecules that make up your body, the atoms that construct the molecules, are traceable to the crucibles that were once the centers of high-mass stars that exploded their chemically rich guts into the galaxy, enriching pristine gas clouds with the chemistry of life. So that we are all connected to each other biologically, to the earth chemically, and to the rest of the universe atomically. . . . We are in the universe and the universe is in us."[13] He adds, "After all, what nobler thought can one cherish than that the universe lives within us all?"[14]

Many years ago, as part of a seminar on creativity and stress management, I led a series of aikido classes (*aikido,* translated as "the way of harmonious energy," is a Japanese martial art) for the Northern Virginia Police Training Academy. The police officers learned to harmonize with various attacks and to redirect the energy. After one of the classes, a grizzled veteran officer whispered in my ear.

"I get it," he said, "This is about becoming a Jedi master."

What is it that gives a Jedi master his powers? The Force. According to the *Urban Dictionary,* "the Force" is "an energy field that binds all living things. It surrounds us, it penetrates us." The Force isn't just a mytho-poetic notion from *Star Wars*. It's real. It is qi. And qi is what gives you mojo.

You don't have to be a mystic, a physicist, or a Jedi to cherish the sense of connection to the universe, and it's more than just a noble thought. *You can learn how to experience it.* We will explore simple, practical ways for you to realize and express this cosmic truth to empower your creativity.

Your Path to Creative Mastery

In part 1 we go right to the heart of qi. For many people, this is the missing link in the fulfillment of their potential. Since 1971, I've been studying how to access and share it. A few years ago, in a moment of revelation, it all came together during an intensive seminar on the ancient Chinese approach to developing this energy, with Robert Peng. While practicing six hours a day, overlooking the Pacific Ocean from a magnificent hilltop in Costa Rica, I experienced an infinite field of pure creative energy and realized that connecting to this source was, more than any technique or tool, the key to creative empowerment. I began to perceive how simple forms of poetic psycho-spiritual choreography could allow us to tap into this pure creative energy, and I started experimenting with new combinations of traditional energy-cultivation exercises.[15]

Part 1, "Mastering Creative Energy," presents the best of what I've learned and created—the simplest, easiest, most potent ways to access and work with this energy. Most of the practices you will learn are from ancient Chinese lineages, because I have found the Chinese approach to be the simplest and most accessible. I've asked masters about their experiences of cultivating, storing, and expressing creative energy and how this energy has benefited their own creativity and that of their students. Then I asked them all to contribute their most powerful practice for cultivating creative energy, something that the average person could do on a typical day, in twenty minutes or less. I searched for what really works, what's universal and not bound by a particular cultural tradition. The words for creative universal energy are different in various traditions—*qi* in China, *ki* (pronounced "key") in Japan, and *prana* in India. But the energy is the same, and it's available to everyone.

The practices you will learn are simple, enjoyable, and effective. If you invest twenty minutes a day, you're likely to discover that within a few months you've significantly strengthened your core creative energy. To make it as easy as possible for you to benefit from these practices you can go to my website, michaelgelb.com, and enjoy free videos to complement your reading.

Part 2 is entitled "Mastering the Creative Mindset." In recent years social science research has confirmed that our attitudes have a profound effect on our performance in a range of abilities, including creativity. *The creative mindset* is my term for the most adaptive, empowering attitudes to strengthen your creativity. You'll learn how to cultivate the energy that supports a creative mindset to raise your effectiveness in all areas of life. Qi is also an acronym for "qualitative impetus," as in the definition of creativity offered in the preface: "the qualitative impetus behind any given act of creation." A creative mindset will raise the qualitative impetus in your life now.

In part 3, "Mastering the Creative Process," we'll illuminate the different modes of thinking that creativity demands. Most people have a habitual, default setting that dominates the way they approach problems. You'll learn how to develop more breadth, depth, originality, and flexibility in your thinking. And you'll learn energy practices that will support your ability to apply the different phases of the creative process in the most elegant and effortless way.

In the finale, entitled "Mastering Creative Energy, Mindset, and Process: Moving from Force to Power," you'll learn a practice that brings together the most important lessons of the book.

If you have a particular creative challenge in your life right now and you're hoping to gain insight and make progress with it, then use that as your focus as you read. If you're just curious about creativity and want to learn the essentials of cultivating it, then relax and explore.

Whatever approach you take, you'll discover that, unlike many other resources, creative energy isn't depleted when you use it.[16] Rather, the more you access it, the stronger it becomes. Although your resources in a given area may be limited, your creativity is potentially infinite, and together, we will explore how to access that unlimited power.

Eckhart Tolle, author of *A New Earth: Awakening to Your Life's Purpose,* observes, "Sustained enthusiasm brings into existence a wave of creative energy, and all you have to do is 'ride the wave.'"[17] I've been riding that wave for forty years, and in this book you'll receive surfing lessons as you learn to tap the vast ocean of creative energy that always surrounds you.

PART 1

MASTERING CREATIVE ENERGY

Genius is mainly an affair of energy.
Matthew Arnold (1822–1888), English poet[1]

C reativity is the mother of all energies," explains Judith Orloff, MD, author of *Positive Energy*. Orloff adds that creativity "is the nurturer of your most alive self. It charges up every part of you. When you're plugged in, a spontaneous combustion occurs that 'artists' don't have a monopoly on."[2]

Yes, there is a boundless source of energy in the universe from which springs all creation and all creativity. Every rock, plant, and animal, including *Homo sapiens,* is a manifestation of its infinite power. Over the course of millennia, humans have been studying how to get directly plugged in to the source of this energy to empower martial prowess, health, and creativity. The oldest record of qi cultivation is an image of a figure, practicing one of the exercises that you will soon learn, on a vase unearthed in China estimated to be more than five thousand years old.

The practices that I will share all originated at a time when the rhythms of nature had much more influence on daily life than they do today. People rose at dawn and retired at sunset. They planted and harvested in harmony with the change of seasons and the movements of the moon and planets.

They watched a heron stalk and then catch a fish.

They observed the praying mantis capturing a fly.

Bears, snakes, monkeys, and cats were their teachers.

They studied the rising and setting of the sun, the waxing and waning of the moon, the flow of water and the patterns of the wind.

They asked: How can I be like the heron and the mantis? What are the secrets of the bear, snake, monkey, and cat? What can I learn from the sun, the moon, the waves, and the wind?

They played. Explored. Danced. Breathed. They experienced qi in all its manifestations and recognized it as their most important natural resource. They experimented to discover how to access, store, and utilize it. Thus, the art of qi cultivation was born.

But these practices arose from more than just shamanic spiritual exploration. These were very practical people. They dug in the earth, stacked hay, moved stones, fought battles. They needed strength and stamina. They had to recover quickly if they were sick or wounded. So they took what they learned from their observations of the natural world and asked: How can we use this to heal? How can we use this to vanquish opponents?

Thus, the healing and martial arts came into being.

And then they contemplated the source of the power behind all creation, and they asked: How can we use this to create?

Feel Qi Now

> I am the taste of pure water and the radiance of the sun
> and moon. I am the sacred word and the sound heard in
> the air and the courage of human beings. I am the sweet
> fragrance in the earth and the radiance of fire.
>
> Bhagavad Gita[3]

Qi is an essential element of our everyday experience. You may notice the flow of qi within you when you enjoy a good yawn or a big belly laugh, or when you experience a sense of refreshment after a shower. You can begin exploring your sensitivity to qi with these two simple practices.

⚡ The Effect of Extrinsic Phenomena on Your Qi

Our qi is affected by external stimuli, for better or worse, every day. If you compare the aroma and taste of a fresh apple with a rotten one you'd immediately, instinctively discern that the fresh one will impart positive life energy while the rotten one might make you sick. Animals in the wild seek out flowing water to drink and avoid stagnant pools for the same reason.

The sonic equivalent of rotten stagnation is expressed masterfully in the album *Metal Machine Music* by Lou Reed (1942–2013). A quick search on your Internet browser will allow you to listen to it. Try any track for as long as you can bear it. Notice the sensations in your body as you listen. Prominent on most lists of the all-time worst music by great artists, this noise will reliably interfere with the qi flow of any sentient being.

Music historians are unsure whether Reed, of Velvet Underground fame, made this album as a joke or as a commentary on the dehumanizing aspects of contemporary life. But it's intriguing to note that before his recent passing, Reed was a devoted student of qi cultivation through tai chi. As he told *Kung Fu Magazine*, "I find tai chi to be philosophically, aesthetically, physically and spiritually fascinating."[4]

Now listen to Reed's classic hit from 1972, "Walk on the Wild Side." Notice the sensations in your body as you listen. Most people report a much more pleasant, uplifting feeling. What is it that depresses or uplifts you when you listen?

The Effect of Intrinsic Phenomena on Your Qi

Besides the food we eat and the sights and sounds we experience, the way we use our body and mind profoundly affects our qi.

Sit in a chair and slump down as though you were depressed. Breathe shallowly through your mouth. Think about something depressing, like Congress, pollution, or income taxes. One minute is more than enough for most people to begin to feel that this posture and attitude impede the normal flow of qi.

Now stand up with your feet shoulder width apart. Align your body around a vertical axis. Smile. Inhale slowly and deeply through your nose, and as you exhale, make an extended *ahhh* sound or a sigh.

Then, keeping your feet firmly on the floor, begin gently shaking your whole body by rhythmically bending and straightening (without locking) your knees. Let your arms flop around as you bounce in a playful and childlike way. Allow your head to move like a buoy bobbing gently on the surface of water.

As you shake, imagine golden light washing through your body, cleansing you of all stress and impurities from head to toe.

After only one minute, almost everyone begins to feel a pleasant tingling sensation. This is a simple way to experience the enlivening of your qi.

Qi Is the Fire of Genius

> There is an electric fire in human nature tending
> to purify—so that among these human creatures there
> is continually some birth of new heroism.
>
> John Keats (1795–1821), English Romantic poet[5]

The common version of the Chinese character for *qi* is a combination of the symbol for rice and the symbol for steam. For the Chinese, rice has long been a primary source of nourishment, and the steam represents the ineffable essence or life force of this sustaining food. But I've always suspected that this was a relatively superficial explanation.

Fortunately, I had the opportunity to ask Ken Cohen about the real meaning of qi. A master of qi cultivation with more than forty-five years' experience, Ken is also a scholar of Chinese language and culture. He explains that the meaning of the term *qi* is expressed more accurately and profoundly in the character that appears in ancient Taoist texts. This character is a combination of the symbol meaning "without" and the symbol for "fire." Ken explains that "without fire" has been misinterpreted to suggest that one must be free from passion to experience enlightenment. Rather, he emphasizes, *qi* is best understood as "the formless fire of life."

Ken explains that cultivating this "formless fire" is, according to ancient Chinese wisdom, the key to creativity in calligraphy, painting, dance, poetry, and music. He says that qi development will make you "a better poet, artist, or performer." He adds, "It also makes you a better, more creative business person."[6]

Qi Is the Real Secret of Creativity

> Tune yourself with the creative power of Spirit. You will be
> in contact with the Infinite Intelligence that is able to guide
> you and to solve all problems. Power from the dynamic
> Source of your being will flow uninterruptedly so that you
> will be able to perform creatively in any sphere of activity.
>
> Paramahansa Yogananda (1893–1952),
> author of Autobiography of a Yogi[7]

Dance legend Martha Graham (1894–1991) was a creative genius. She revolutionized modern dance and influenced many great terpsichoreans, including Alvin Ailey, Merce Cunningham, Erick Hawkins, Paul Taylor, and Twyla Tharp. Graham captured a profound truth about the essence of creativity when she said, "There is a vitality, a life force, an energy, a quickening that is translated through you into action, and because there is only one of you in all of time, this expression is unique." She added, "[I]f you block it, it will never exist through any other medium and it will be lost. . . . It is not your business to determine how good it is . . . nor how it compares with other expressions. It is your business to keep it yours clearly and directly, to keep the channel open. You do not even have to believe in yourself or your work. You have to keep yourself open and aware to the urges that motivate you. Keep the channel open."[8]

The vitality, life force, energy, quickening that you translate into action is qi. And it's not hard to recognize.

Consider a work of art that has moved you deeply. Whether it's a play, a musical composition, a painting, or a dance, chances are that, more than the words, notes, colors, or choreography, you were affected most by the *energy* of the piece. As musician and teacher of "Qi for Creativity" John Voigt explains, "What makes any art great is the use and communication of the energy of life. Most listeners, viewers, readers only subliminally sense this vitality. They do not know it in the verbal part of their minds, but they demand it from any art they choose to experience. Without that life energy—what we call *qi*—any art is lifeless, academic, weak."[9]

In traditional Chinese landscape painting, artists aimed to convey the experience of this vivifying force. Osvald Sirén (1879–1966), author of *The Chinese on the Art of Painting*, explains that the power of qi is "something that links the works of the individual artist with a cosmic principle." He adds that it is "active in the artist before it becomes manifest in his works; it is like an echo from the divine part of his creative genius reverberating in lines and shapes which he draws with his hand. . . . [I]t manifests unconsciously and spreads like a flash over the picture."[10]

In his history of heroes of the imagination, entitled *The Creators*, Daniel J. Boorstin (1914–2004) cites T'ang Hou, an ancient Chinese philosopher of art who explains that the artist must align with "the shaping powers of Nature" so that "the charm of inexhaustible transformation is unfailingly visible." T'ang Hou adds, "If you yourself do not possess that grand wavelike vastness of mountain and valley within your heart and mind, you will be unable to capture it with ease in your painting."[11]

You were born from "grand wavelike vastness"; it is your true nature, and reconnecting with it will revivify your creativity in all areas of life. Besides being the secret of great art, vibrant qi is the key to a delicious meal, an engaging presentation, a fulfilling experience of making love, and a successful entrepreneurial venture.

This insight into the source of creativity isn't solely the province of the East. American philosopher Ralph Waldo Emerson (1803–1882) describes a secret learned by every wise individual: "[B]eyond the energy of his . . . conscious intellect, he is capable of a new energy by abandonment to the nature of things; that, beside his privacy of power as an individual man, there is a great public power, on which he can draw, by unlocking his human doors, and suffering the ethereal tides to roll and circulate through him: then he is caught up into the life of the Universe, his speech is thunder, his thought is law."[12]

Emerson advises us to discover new energy by "abandonment to the nature of things," by "unlocking our human doors" and allowing "the ethereal tides to roll and circulate" within, to participate more fully in the life of the universe. If we do, our "thought is law"—in other words, what we envision is created.

The ability to roll and circulate the ethereal tides, to keep the channel open, to move and direct the flow of qi, and to experience the charm of inexhaustible transformation is the secret of great art and a creative life.

Creators on Qi

Carol Rose Brown

Through my exploration of qi cultivation I've met many exceptionally creative people. I've asked many of them what qi means and how it informs their creative process. I've included some of the responses throughout the book, in sidebars entitled "Creators on Qi." Here's one from an artist in my Santa Fe qi-cultivation class.

Carol Rose Brown is a gifted painter of the natural world and has a special talent for expressing the numinous quality in her subjects. She took a long time to respond to my question about the way qi informs her art because like many true creators she is genuinely humble and on some level knows that she is more of a conduit than a source. Carol eventually wrote:

> I began practicing meditation, tai chi, and other methods for nourishing qi a long time ago, and the longer I do it the more I feel there's nothing I can say about it. I don't know much about it. I've been reading about qi since I was in college and first picked up *The Mustard Seed Garden Manual of Painting,* the Chinese guide for painters that urged them to become the tree before they put the brush to the scroll.
>
> The only thing I can say is: when I draw something—say the aspens turning on the mountain—and the landscape just whooshes through my eyes into the pencil onto the paper, and I just sit there watching the drawing happening but not doing anything, that's when I feel I've connected with qi.[13]

Basic Qi Principles

Let's consider a few basic insights that will help you get the most from the qi-cultivation practices in this book.

Your Body Is an Antenna for Qi

> I love to think of nature as having unlimited broadcasting stations,
> through which God speaks to us every day, every hour
> and every moment of our lives, if we will only tune in.
> George Washington Carver (1864–1943), American scientist[14]

Your body is an antenna for qi, and your mind can direct the antenna to get better reception. As George Washington Carver counsels, all we need to do is tune in and listen to the broadcast. The qi-cultivation practices you will learn in this book will put you on the right creative wavelength.

Qi Responds to Your Intention and Imagination

Indeed, the power of imagination makes us infinite.

John Muir (1838–1914),
Scottish-American naturalist and founder of the Sierra Club[15]

Creative visualization is a well-documented way to improve performance in a wide range of activities, from martial arts to free-throw shooting. In a recent study entitled "Mind Over Matter: Mental Training Increases Physical Strength," Erin M. Shackell and Lionel G. Standing demonstrated that "mental practice" resulted in significant gains in strength for their subjects who were college athletes. Moreover, their survey of hundreds of research papers in the field led them to conclude, "mental practice produces measurable gains in skilled performance."[16]

The same thing is true with qi. Just as you can strengthen your muscles or improve your free-throw shooting by using your imagination creatively, you can also access, circulate, and store qi by directing it with your intention and imagination.

Qi Flows Naturally and Effortlessly

Don't push the river; it flows by itself.

Ancient proverb[17]

The primary focus of the practices you will learn is letting go of interference with the natural flow of qi. Like wind blowing around a mountain or water flowing toward the ocean, qi follows the path of least resistance. As you harmonize with and encourage the natural movements of qi, you experience greater ease and flow in all of your activities.

Graceful Movements Invite the Energy of Grace

> Grace is the beauty of form under the influence of freedom.
>
> Friedrich Schiller (1759–1805), German philosopher and poet[18]

Awkward, violent, and crass movements activate energies that are awkward, violent, and crass. Graceful movements invite the flow of grace. Perform the movements with a sense of flow, ease, and joy and you will get the most benefit. And you can dramatically enhance the flow of qi in your daily life by bringing more poise and grace to your everyday movements.

When doing movement practices, invest special attention to the transition between one movement and another. When you bring mindfulness to the space between movements, you create an energetic continuity that enhances the pleasure and the benefits.

You Don't Have to Believe the Metaphysics
to Get the Benefits of Qi

> I don't believe in anything you have to believe in.
>
> Fran Lebowitz, American author and critic[19]

You don't need to believe in qi to get the benefits of the practices. All you need is an open mind. If you experiment with the practices, you will almost certainly feel better. If you prefer, you can think of them as poetic choreography designed to facilitate an experience of creative empowerment. And if you follow a religious or spiritual path, you can customize the practices to reinforce and support that path.

Devoting Your Full Attention
to the Qi Practices Makes Them Work

> Living in the now will be the wave of the future.
>
> Swami Beyondananda, American humorist[20]

The practices that you will learn can all be done in twenty minutes or less. They will all give you the maximum experience of qi in the shortest possible time. For that time to be worthwhile, you must devote your full attention to each one as you do it. As you savor every moment of movement and breath, you'll discover that movement and breath are always, only, ever, happening *now*. And in the now you can experience your connection to eternal qi, the source of creativity. "Forever," as Emily Dickinson reminds us, "is composed of nows."[21]

Your Body Is an Energy Transformer

> Everyone should consider his body as a priceless gift from one whom
> he loves above all, a marvelous work of art, of indescribable beauty,
> and mystery beyond human conception.
>
> Nikola Tesla (1856–1943), Serbian-American inventor and futurist[22]

An aspiring qi master is visiting New York City.

He walks up to a hot dog stand and asks, "Please make me one with everything."

The vendor creates a hot dog with sauerkraut, mustard, chili, and bacon—everything—and hands it to the hungry adept, who pays with a $20 bill. The vendor puts the bill in his pocket.

"Where's my change?" asks the fledging master.

The vendor responds, "Change comes from within."

The ability to create, and to make creative changes in your life, is within you. It is your birthright. You can use it any way you desire. And it helps to understand that your body, in addition to being an antenna for qi, is also designed as an energy-transformation medium. We know, for example, that when we eat a hot dog we transform the calories into fuel for our daily lives. We can do something similar with qi, to fuel our creativity and spiritual development.

The way you think, breathe, and behave determines the amplitude and frequency with which the qi vibrates within. Imagine how much more creative you can be as you bring more mindfulness to the flow of your energy and learn how to transform it into vibratory patterns that are more in alignment with your creative purpose.

Prepare for Better Reception:
Assuming Your Full Stature

When I was in eighth grade, I had a wonderfully eccentric Irish-American math teacher named Miss Moran. She was an old-school schoolmarm who drilled us mercilessly on the basics of algebra. While facing the blackboard, she would sense that we were all slumping in our chairs, and she would intone, in a shrill, unforgettable voice, the command "Postures!" We snapped to attention as she whipped around to inspect our compliance.

When she faced the blackboard again, we resumed slumping. Nevertheless, Miss Moran made a lasting impression. She understood something that I would realize many years later: *our state of attention is reflected in the body's alignment, and an upright alignment is critical to the refinement of attention.*

Every tradition for accessing creative universal energy emphasizes the importance of an upright alignment: Zen Buddhist meditators, Hindu yogis, and tai chi masters all teach the upright posture as the first step in aligning with the creative universal energy. There's no sustained tradition in the world that suggests we begin our practice by slumping, collapsing, or distorting our posture.

In 1980 I traveled to South Africa, where I interviewed the anthropologist and anatomist Raymond Dart (1893–1988), renowned for his discovery of the so-called missing link in human evolution. When asked for his advice on the development of human potential, Dart, who was eighty-seven years old at the time, leapt out of his chair and exclaimed, "Balance! Balance the mind. Balance the body. Balance is the key."

Dart developed a series of movements designed to help us cultivate balance and understand the relationship between our upright stature and our potential for awareness. The following practice is adapted from Dart's teaching.

You can do this practice by yourself, but it's even more fun with a group. I've led this practice for groups around the world, and there's something about acting the role of earlier stages of evolution that helps people connect with one another. It will also deepen your appreciation of the relationship between your upright stature and your consciousness.

The Evolution of Consciousness in Ten Minutes

Place a towel or yoga mat on the floor and begin by lying face down. If it's not too uncomfortable, experiment with touching your forehead to the floor, or let your head rest to the left or right. Place your arms alongside your body, with the back of your palms on the floor.

Relax for a minute in this unusual posture. Enjoy the experience of support from the ground. Here, there is no fear of falling! As you relax, contemplate the consciousness that is possible from this worldview of a primordial creature. Your mindset is limited to seeking food, guided by your sense of smell. Your wiggling is all you have to propel your mouth forward to feed.

Now prepare for a major leap forward in evolution. Drag the backs of your palms up alongside your torso until you have to flip them over, and place your palms flat on the floor so that your elbows are just under your shoulders. Your forearms also rest on the floor. Enjoy a full, deep inhalation. As you exhale, press down on your palms to raise your head and neck up off the floor. (This posture is known as the Sphinx in yoga practice.)

Allow your whole spine to continue lengthening gently as you look around from your new vantage point, reflecting on the differences in consciousness that are now possible, compared to your earlier evolutionary phase.

Next, shift your body up onto all fours. Place your hands flat on the floor directly underneath your shoulders, with your knees just underneath your hips. You've just recapitulated many millions of years of evolution, moving from a reptilian world into the mammalian realm. Take a few moments to look around from this angle and notice the difference in your possibilities for awareness.

Explore the mammalian realm by exhaling as you arch your spine, raising your middle back up into the air. Look down toward your belly and curl your tailbone forward toward your nose. Then, as you inhale, allow your middle back to sink and arch the other way; your eyes are looking up to the ceiling, and your tailbone pointing up toward the ceiling as well. (In yoga, these two postures are known as Cat and Cow.)

Move back and forth between these two positions, moving in harmony with your breathing, seven times. Take your time and savor each position and the transfer between them. This delightful movement encourages the attunement, flexibility, and balance of your spine and central energy channel.

Now take the next profound evolutionary leap by coming up into a primate stance. Shift your weight onto your feet, with your knees and hips bent. Bring your hands off the floor and allow your arms to swing freely. Your spine is angled forward from your hips. Imagining yourself as a chimpanzee, gorilla, orangutan, or other primate, contemplate the possibilities of consciousness as you "monkey around."

After enjoying the simian state for a minute (or longer if you like), slowly raise yourself up to human stature. Stand at your full height, creating the maximum distance between your feet and the top of your head.

Contemplate the consciousness that is now available to you. Feel your potential for greater awareness and freedom. Your ability to quickly turn 360 degrees allows you to scan what surrounds you with much greater ease. Your arms and hands are much freer, making it possible for you to conduct an orchestra or paint a picture. But notice also the relative vulnerability that comes with the freedom. The risk level for falling has increased dramatically. This vulnerability can lead us to contract, shorten our stature, and reverse our evolutionary progress.

Assuming your full stature is the first essential practice for cultivating qi. It aligns the flow of energy within you with the flows of
energy that are all around you. A fully upright posture enhances
your receptivity and your ability to store, circulate, and express qi.
Aligning yourself this way is the key to tuning your antenna.

Basic Energy Anatomy and Terminology

Energy is eternal delight.

William Blake (1757–1827), English visionary, poet, and painter[23]

A full understanding of internal energy anatomy requires years of study.
Fortunately, you can get great benefit from the practices you will learn
here with just a bit of rudimentary knowledge. Here are the basics:

The central channel. The most important energy pathway,
running from the center of the top of your head straight
through the center of your body to the perineum. This channel
corresponds to the vertical axis of your body.

The apex. This is the point on the crown of the head that is the
top, or apex, of the central channel. This point is a powerful
conduit for connecting your personal energy with cosmic energy.

The base. This point at the bottom of the torso is the bottom,
or base, of the central channel. A plumb line straight down
through the center of your body from the apex would touch
this spot at the center of the pelvic floor, also known as the
perineum. This point is a powerful conduit for connecting your
personal energy with the energy of the earth.

The left and right channels. Energy pathways that flow on both
sides of the central channel. These pathways are sometimes

called "sun" and "moon," but we will just refer to them as left and right.

The three centers. Known as "elixir fields" in Chinese, these centers are major reservoirs for qi. **Upper:** The thinking center, this is the area radiating out from the center of your brain. **Middle:** The feeling center, this is the area radiating out from the center of your solar plexus. **Lower:** The instinctive center, this is the area radiating out from a point three inches below your navel. It corresponds roughly with your center of gravity.

The Three Treasures. In Taoist philosophy, humans serve as a bridge between the energies of heaven and earth. The Three Treasures are the energies of these three domains: celestial, earthly, and human. The three centers (see above) serve as reservoirs for qi; they vibrate at different but complementary frequencies. The lower center is the primary point of alignment with earth qi. The middle center is the main storehouse of human qi. And the upper center is the key antenna for celestial qi. Many qi-cultivation practices aim to facilitate a blending and transformation of the energies that always surround us (celestial and earth) with the human energy that is our birthright.

Prenatal and acquired qi. We are all born with an inheritance of qi, an endowment of fundamental life energy. The Chinese refer to this as prenatal qi. And we can, through a healthy lifestyle and conscious practice, cultivate our qi. This is known as acquired qi.

The point of perception. The point at the center of your forehead, between your eyebrows, also known as the third eye.

The shoulder nests. If you round your shoulder girdle forward on either side and feel into the deepest part of the indentation created by that movement, you will discover your shoulder nests.

The hip creases. These are the creases between your upper thigh and your hip joint. The shoulder nests and hip creases are key junction points in the flow of energy along the left and right channels.

The heart of the palms. If you trace a line down your middle finger and another across from the place where the top of your thumb joins the rest of your hand, you'll discover the heart of the palm at the intersection. These points are conduits for healing and martial qi.

The Bubbling Springs. If you massage the area just behind the ball of your foot, in the center, you'll discover the Bubbling Spring. These points connect you to the energy of the earth.

The Jade Pillow. The place where your neck ends and your head begins, at the base of the occiput.

The palatal junction. Whisper the words "Let go." Notice how, as you pronounce the first syllable, your tongue touches your palate gently. The point where your tongue touches your palate is the junction that connects the upward-flowing energy that runs up your back with the downward-flowing energy that flows down the front. This entire circular pathway is known as the "microcosmic orbit" or the "small heavenly circuit." When you practice qi cultivation, or at any time during the day when it occurs to you, place your tongue on the roof of your mouth in this way. This helps to harmonize the qi flow throughout your system.

The aura. *Urban Dictionary* defines it as "the ever-changing flow of life energy around one's body." It adds, "It can be harnessed for supernatural abilities, though not as extreme as showcased in some animes (i.e., Dragonball Z)." The aura is sometimes referred to as our energy field.

Qigong. *Gong* is a Chinese word that can be translated as "cultivation" or "workout." Qigong, then, is a "workout for qi" or simply qi cultivation.

Tai chi chuan. The phrase *tai chi chuan* literally translates as "supreme ultimate fist." Commonly referred to as just tai chi, it is a popular form of martial art and healing exercise.

Using Everyday Activities to Cultivate Your Qi

You can easily enhance your receptivity to qi by shifting your perspective on five things you already do every day: lying down, standing, sitting, walking, and breathing. Lying down, standing, sitting, and walking are known in some ancient traditions as the "Four Dignities of Humanity." I've added breathing as the fifth.

Lying Down

Sometimes, after a long day of teaching, followed by a client dinner, I get back to my hotel room and I'm tempted to just collapse on the bed. I've learned instead to lie down gracefully, stretch my arms and legs out at comfortable angles, and simply open to the restorative power of qi. It helps to allow the palms to face upward, to receive more energy through the heart of the palms. I close my eyes and allow long, slow breaths into my belly.

At the end of most yoga classes, everyone rests in a posture known as *savasana,* or Corpse Pose. This is the most important pose in yoga practice, because it allows for an integration of the energies generated by the yoga postures and movements. But you don't have to take a yoga class beforehand to benefit from doing it. Your work can be thought of as a form of yoga practice, and ending your workday with this pose will integrate the learning of your day and restore your qi.

⚡ Central Channel Tune-Up

Here's another elegant lying-down practice—a great way to tune up your spine and central energy channel.[24] All you need to begin is a quiet place, some carpeted floor space or a yoga mat, a few paperback books, and fifteen to twenty minutes.

Begin by stacking the books on the floor. Stand approximately your body's length away from the books, facing away from them, with your feet shoulder width apart. Let your hands rest gently at your sides. Look straight ahead with a soft focus.

Direct your apex point up to heaven. Become aware of your feet on the floor and an energetic connection with the ground through your Bubbling Spring points. Notice the distance from your feet to the top of your head. Listen to the sounds around you.

Moving lightly and easily, lower yourself onto the floor. Supporting yourself with your hands behind you, bend your knees and place your feet flat on the floor in front of you. Keep your spine as upright as possible without straining. Continue breathing easily. Let your head drop forward a bit to ensure that you are not tightening your neck muscles and pulling your head back.

Gently lower your spine, vertebra by vertebra, onto the floor so that your head comes to rest on the books. The books should be positioned so that they support your head at the place where your neck ends and your head begins (the Jade Pillow). If your head is not well positioned, reach back with one hand and support your head while using the other hand to place the books in the proper position. Add or take books away until you find a height that encourages a gentle lengthening of your neck muscles.

Your feet remain flat on the floor, your knees point up to the ceiling, and your arms are by your sides. Your hands can rest on the floor or be loosely folded on your chest. Allow the weight of your body to be fully supported by the floor. (See figure 1.1.)

Rest in this position for fifteen to twenty minutes. As you rest, gravity will be lengthening your spine and realigning your torso. Keep your eyes open to avoid dozing off. Bring your attention to the flow of your breathing and to the gentle pulsation of your whole body. Be aware of the ground supporting your back, and allow your shoulders to rest as your back widens.

After you have rested for fifteen to twenty minutes, you will get up slowly, being careful to avoid stiffening or shortening your body as you return to a standing position. In order to enjoy a smooth transition, decide when you are going to move and then gently roll over onto your front, maintaining your new sense of integration and expansion. Ease yourself onto your hands and knees, and then up onto one knee. With your head leading the movement upward, stand up.

Pause for a few moments, eyes alert. Listen. Again, feel your feet on the floor, and notice the distance between your feet and the apex.

figure 1.1 Central Channel Tune-Up

You may be delighted to discover that the distance has expanded. As you move into the activities of your day, think about not doing anything that interferes with this expansion, ease, and uplift.[25]

Standing

Qi master and martial artist Ken Cohen describes his teacher, Master Chan: "He was soft and flexible, like water, but he could hit like a tidal wave. His grip was like a powerful steel vise."[26] Ken was curious about the source of his teacher's prowess. He reflects:

> I had probably watched too many martial arts movies. I imagined that he did finger pushups and spent hours each day slapping bricks and thrusting his fingers into heated sand.
>
> One day, I asked him, "Why are your fingers so strong?"
>
> He immediately dropped into a low squat and struck his fingers full force onto the concrete floor. Then he stood up, rolled and tapped his fingers in the air, and said, "You see, no pain, and I can still play piano."
>
> "Yes, I can see that," I said, "But how?"
>
> He replied, "You won't believe me," whereupon he bent his knees and raised his arms into a rounded shape, as though embracing a tree. "Standing," he said, "is the secret."[27]

Standing is, as Ken learned from his teacher, a profoundly powerful practice. I first learned standing as a qi practice from Master Shuren Ma many years ago. At my first class we were instructed to stand with a lengthening spine, knees bent and eyes closed. As an athlete and martial artist, I thought this would be easy, but after about ten minutes I started to shake and discovered all kinds of tensions that I didn't know I had. Master Ma came over and gently touched my wrist. Suddenly, the shaking vanished, and I was able to stand comfortably for another ten minutes. When the class finished, I felt amazingly energized.

Master Chan explained why we shake: "It means that there's water in the pressure cooker, but the lid is not properly sealed or tight—it is bobbing up and down. In other words, your body is not yet strong or stable enough to hold the qi."[28]

As you practice standing meditation, you become a stronger and more stable container for qi. And a skilled teacher can help you allow the flow of qi, as Master Ma did for me, with a well-placed and sensitive touch.

In recovering from joint-replacement surgery, I've used standing meditation as a core healing practice. When I first started post-surgery, I could barely do five minutes, and now I'm comfortable for an hour. Standing meditation has done more for my strength and balance than all the physical therapy exercises I did put together. For the purpose of creative empowerment, I recommend *gradually* working your way up to a twenty-minute practice. After twenty minutes of standing, you will feel the buildup of a reserve of qi that you can use to express yourself creatively.

In addition to the formal standing meditation practice, there are many opportunities to use standing to attune yourself to qi. Whether you're waiting in line at the grocery store, an airport gate, or the bank, or even attending a cocktail party, you can make your standing mindful and open yourself to receive the qi that is always present.

Simple Standing Meditation

The basic standing posture of this meditation is also the basis for several other practices. There are many variations of standing meditation that employ different positions of the arms and hands, but this most basic one, which can be done unobtrusively in public, allows your hands to rest at your sides.

The Basic Standing Posture
Stand with your feet parallel and spaced shoulder width apart. Distribute your weight evenly through both feet.

Align around your vertical axis: Keep the apex and base points in one line. Let your spine be supple, like the trunk of a willow tree. Feel the weight of your jaw and shoulders. As you sense their weight, they relax.

Allow your lower back, sacrum, and tailbone to release downward, toward the ground, as you direct the apex point up to the sky. Soften the hip creases and allow your knees to bend slightly. (Keep your knees in line with your big toes and avoid allowing the knees to bend past the big toes.)

Rest your hands at your sides, maintaining a gentle curve through your elbows, and allow there to be space between each of your fingers. (See figure 1.2.)

Gently rest your tongue on the palatal junction point.

The Meditation

In formal practice, you can close your eyes. When practicing informally in public, keep your eyes open and soften your gaze so that you take in both the central and peripheral focus. Smile. Maintain an attitude of openness, receptivity, and gratitude.

Imagine that qi is permeating your entire being, entering through all the pores of your skin and nurturing every cell of your body. Concentrate the qi into your central channel as you inhale, and then extend your central channel up to the sky and down to the earth as you exhale.

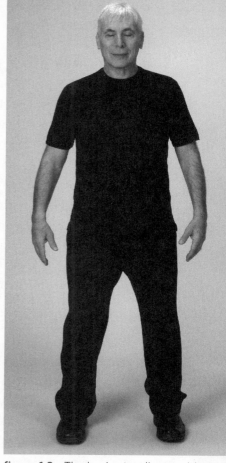

figure 1.2 The basic standing position

Sitting

A recent study by Denmark's National Institute of Public Health demonstrated that people who sit for more than six hours a day might lose up to seven years of life expectancy.[29] Other studies have shown higher risks for cancer and heart disease among those who sit for extended periods. What these studies didn't consider is *how* people sit. Chances are that the sedentary subjects in the study weren't sitting aligned around their vertical axis, and they probably weren't circulating their qi.

Even if you sit properly, it's a good idea to get up and walk for a minute or two every twenty or thirty minutes. And you can make a major positive difference to your baseline level of qi by sitting intelligently. How? Imagine that you are sitting at your desk and the person that you admire most in the world walks into the room. How would your posture change? You'd probably lengthen your spine, sit up, and brighten your eyes. The simple explanation of how to sit is to do it as though you were always with the person you admire most. Here are a few points to remember:

- Sit with your feet flat on the ground. This provides a balanced platform and grounds your energy. If your feet don't reach the ground, then place a box on the floor and rest your feet on the box.
- Keep your knees lower than your hips. When your knees are higher than your hips, there's a tendency for the hip joints to contract and become jammed physically and energetically. If you have long legs, you may need to add a seat cushion to raise your torso in relation to your legs.
- Align around the vertical axis. Maintain the maximum distance from your base to your apex.

If you make it a habit to sit upright, you'll discover that you have more energy and mental clarity throughout the day.

Sitting mindfully, with poise in an upright position, is the essence of seated meditation. When you sit with dignity, you are tuning the qi antenna. Prior to any important creative endeavor, sit quietly for *Breathe* twenty minutes, following the flow of your breathing. As you inhale, • breathe in the qi and allow it to fill every cell of your being; as you exhale, let go of anything that prevents you from being fully receptive. As Paramahansa Yogananda advises, "Before embarking on important undertakings, sit quietly, calm your senses and thoughts, and meditate deeply. You will then be guided by the great creative power of Spirit."[30]

Yogananda's advice is supported by contemporary scientific research. In a recent article entitled "Meditation Makes You More Creative," *Science Daily* reported on a study at Leiden University in the Netherlands.[31] The study showed that a form of open-focus mindfulness meditation resulted in improvements in subjects' ability to generate ideas and make connections between seemingly unrelated ideas.[32]

Richard J. Davidson, PhD, founder and chair of the Center for Investigating Healthy Minds at the University of Wisconsin–Madison and coauthor of *The Emotional Life of Your Brain,* has maintained his own personal meditation practice for many years. He comments:

> Although much more research needs to be done for us to understand the relationship between meditation and creativity, we have established that many positive changes in the brain can be nurtured through mindfulness training. In my experience, sitting in meditation can be a profound and effective aid for the creative process. Our perspective broadens, the stickiness of our thoughts and emotions declines and we become acutely aware of the broad range of connections and associations our minds make. This is the stuff from which creative insights bubble and the awareness that mindfulness cultivates can help us to harness and retain the insights that arise.[33]

Walking

Walk as if you are kissing the Earth with your feet.

Thich Nhat Hanh, Vietnamese Zen Buddhist teacher and author[34]

Walking is the preferred form of exercise for many of history's greatest geniuses. Thomas Jefferson called it "the best possible exercise."[35] Walking has also been cherished through the ages as a means to facilitate creative insight. *Solvitur ambulando* is the Latin phrase meaning "It is solved by walking." Philosopher and poet Henry David Thoreau (1817–1862) expressed it thusly: "Me thinks that the moment my legs begin to move, my thoughts begin to flow."[36]

Julia Cameron, author of *The Artist's Way*, recommends a dedicated solo walk once a week as an essential practice for cultivating creativity. She explains, "All large change is made through many small steps. Notice that word in there—'step.' Walking leads us a step at a time."[37] Cameron emphasizes that walking is a gentle, easy way to deepen our creative reception and open to inner guidance.

I agree. And you can enhance the benefits of walking in terms of both creativity and health with a simple practice to become even more receptive to qi.

I learned the following qi walking practice from Robert Peng, who learned it while walking with his master in a mountainous region of China. During their walks, Robert's master brought his attention to the craftspeople of the local village. These artisans worked to handcraft beautiful furniture and then carry it on their backs over steep mountain passes to the marketplace miles away. Robert was amazed by their ability to shoulder these heavy loads for miles uphill without exhaustion.

"The amazing thing is that as soon as they would stop, they resumed their normal breathing very quickly," he said. "What was their secret? Every now and then, for about ten to twenty minutes, they did a special breathing practice that gave them this exceptional power."[38]

Simple Qi Walking Practice

This practice makes walking even more enjoyable and inspiring.

You can do this practice for up to twenty minutes at a time. You will be inhaling through your nose and exhaling through your mouth. (If the air is very cold or dry, you might prefer to inhale through your mouth or through both nose and mouth together.)

As you inhale, rotate your thumbs away from your body to gently open your arms, allowing your palms to open to receive qi from around you. (If you are practicing in public, walking down a busy street or through a crowded airport, you can make the hand movements very subtle so that no one notices.)

When you exhale, rotate your thumbs back toward your body, turning your palms inward, and imagine that you are pumping qi down to the Bubbling Spring points in your feet. Also as you exhale, push the air up against the upper palate as though you were whispering the word *who* loudly. Emphasize the "whispered *who*" more strongly on the second part of the exhalation.

Enjoy a qi walk, devoted solely to the notion of enhancing your creative receptivity, at least once a week.

Breathing

> Breath is the thread that ties creation together.
>
> Morihei Ueshiba (1883–1969),
> Japanese martial artist, founder of aikido[39]

Breathing is a practice that you are always doing, consciously or not. There are myriad ways of using the breath to intensify your connection with qi; many of them are complex and best practiced under the direct guidance of a master. Here are some general guidelines that can help you get the most out of every breath:

- If you can, breathe in through your nose. Exhale through either your nose or mouth.

- Breathe into your belly. As qi master Frank Allen emphasized to me, "When you breathe into your belly, allow your whole waist to expand. In other words, include your lower back and your sides in the expansion."
- Avoid interfering with your breathing as you move. Many people hold their breath in everyday movements, such as rising from a chair, turning a steering wheel, or brushing their teeth. When you inadvertently hold your breath, you send a stress signal throughout your mind and body.
- Draw in the pure creative energy of the universe as you inhale. As you exhale, let go of anything that interferes with your full aliveness.
- When in doubt, exhale.

Slow, easy, mindful breathing opens a gateway to deeper creative awareness. When we breathe in a deep, natural, rhythmic way, life unfolds out of the eternal present, and the mind is freed to be more spontaneous and open.

Ken Cohen offers an exquisitely simple approach to harmonizing respiration in a way that helps us access the alpha and theta brainwave pattern associated with creativity. Drawn from an ancient practice called Embryonic Respiration, you'll breathe in a gentle, effortless, and innocent way, as though you've returned to the safety of the womb.

Embryonic Breathing Meditation

You can do this practice lying down, sitting, or standing. The meditation is best learned in three easy phases. Explore each phase in turn for approximately eight cycles of breath (one inhale plus one exhale equals one cycle), and then put all three phases together for ten to twenty minutes to experience blissful serenity.

Phase 1: Engaging in Basic Qi Breathing

As you inhale through your nose, your belly expands gently. When you exhale, it releases. With each inhalation, allow the pure creative energy of the universe to fill your entire being. As you exhale, let go of anything that interferes with your full aliveness.

Phase 2: Savoring the Four Stages of the Breath Cycle

The four stages are (1) the inhale, (2) the turning of the breath before exhalation, (3) the exhale, and (4) the turning of the breath before inhalation. In this phase, you will direct your attention to each in turn.

Breathe in easily and then notice the moment when the breath turns from inhale to exhale. The breath then releases effortlessly and is followed by the sensation that the next breath is ready to come in. As you bring your attention to the transitions between inhaling and exhaling, and allow those moments to be frictionless, like the rolling of the tide, you'll discover that your breath slows and becomes more rhythmic.

Phase 3: Cultivating the Five Qualities

Once you've experienced the harmony of the four stages of the breath cycle, you can begin to cultivate five qualities that will lead to a blissful state of creative potentiality: slow, long, deep, smooth, and even.

Cohen explains, "The breath is slow—that is, not hurried or anxious. The breath is long, like a long river flowing on and on. The breath is deep, sinking low in the body, all the way to the abdomen, or you may even feel it dropping all the way into your feet or the ground. The breath is smooth, like silk. And the breath is even; you do not favor any particular stage of the breath. Inhale and exhale flow one into the next."

He continues, "As you practice [the five qualities], your breath will become exceedingly slow and gentle. If you held a down feather in front of the nostrils, perhaps it would not move." Cohen adds, "While practicing Embryonic Breathing, you may feel as though your body has become one with the creative-energy universe."[40]

Qi-Cultivation Practices

From the living fountain of instinct flows everything that is creative.
C. G. Jung (1875–1961),
Swiss psychiatrist, founder of analytical psychology[41]

Although these practices are simple, easy, and pleasurable, they are profoundly powerful. They represent the distilled wisdom of some of the world's great masters of creative energy. When I teach these practices in a workshop, we usually devote at least three hours to introducing each one. So it's best not to do them all in sequence, one after the other, as this could be overwhelming.

Instead, read through them at your leisure and notice which ones appeal to you the most. Experiment with those that call to you, and then you can explore others.

Again, each practice can be completed in twenty minutes or less. They don't require any special equipment or venue. You can do them at home, in your office, in a hotel room, on airplanes, and in airports—anywhere, anytime. Some people like to practice upon arising, and others prefer the end of the day. Experiment to discover what works best for you. You will find, however, that if you must work on a creative project, you will be far more productive if you do a practice before beginning work.

Unlike exercise you might do at the gym, these practices don't depend on stressing the muscles or the cardiovascular system for their positive effects. Rather, they work by encouraging the natural movement of qi within your body and between your body and the unlimited field of energy that surrounds you. As you enjoy the graceful movements, breathing patterns, and visualizations in these practices, you'll discover an empowerment of your "living fountain of instinct," as Jung called it, from which flows all creativity. These practices will put you in neurophysiological states that are conducive to creating. If you practice just twenty minutes each day, you'll soon notice that you are becoming more attuned to your intuition.

If you practice regularly, you will also probably experience long-term benefits in creative empowerment and wellness, and you'll also discover that practice makes you feel good right away.

For best results, approach each practice with a lighthearted, experimental, and playful attitude. Your mindset is the most important aspect of qi cultivation. Avoid worrying about getting the movements perfectly correct. Focus instead on gently encouraging the flow of your qi. *You can get the full benefits of the practices even if you are unable to do the physical movements.* Just imagine the movements and coordinate your breathing with the imagined movements to the best of your ability, and you'll discover that your qi begins to move.

Nourishing Your Qi

> I have felt . . . a sense sublime
> Of something far more deeply interfused,
> Whose dwelling is the light of setting suns,
> And the round ocean and the living air,
> And the blue sky, and in the mind of man;
> A motion and a spirit, that impels
> All thinking things, all objects of all thought,
> And rolls through all things.
>
> William Wordsworth (1770–1850), English Romantic poet[42]

The simplest and perhaps the most powerful practice of all is to open your self to the motion and spirit of qi. At any given moment—like now, for example—you can embrace an attitude of receptivity to this sublime energy and imagine it rolling through every fiber of your being. Robert Peng explains how his teacher initiated him into this practice:

When my master first told me I had to "do qigong
twenty-hour hours a day," I felt very confused and
frustrated. Eventually, he explained that when I wasn't
actively cultivating qi through a specific practice I could,
nevertheless, continue to multiply the benefits. He said:
"All these days you are working on qi, you should allow the
qi to work on you! The qi has much better intelligence than
you. Just relax and allow the qi to seep into every cell in
your body like a sponge soaking in warm water, and it will
do an amazing job for you."[43]

You can practice nourishing your qi anywhere, at any time. If you like, you can repeat a phrase that helps you remember that you are deeply interfused with the creative energy of the universe: "I am in qi. Qi is in me." And you'll get even more benefit from all the practices if you spend a minute or two after each one just nourishing your qi.

Three Treasures Standing Meditation

Beginning in October of 1973, I spent ten months on a residential retreat studying with mathematician, philosopher, and spiritual guide J. G. Bennett (1897–1974). Bennett taught a simple but profound way of understanding ourselves and one another. Human beings, he said, have three centers or brains: the physical (gut), emotional (heart), and intellectual (cerebral cortex). Due to our unnatural and artificial living conditions, most people function with a dis-coordination of these three centers. Bennett emphasized the importance of developing all three centers and harmonizing them into a conscious, integrated, creative, and continuously evolving self.

Since that time, I've sought to empower and integrate my intellect, emotions, physicality, and spirit. This integration has a profoundly positive effect on creativity. Empowering the center of intellect and wisdom, we open ourselves to greater creative inspiration. As we nurture the heart, we enhance the likelihood that what we create will be offered in a context of service and compassion. As we enliven the center of our physical vitality, we strengthen our ability to follow through and implement our creative dreams. We bring these three centers into coordinated action by aligning them with our spirit.

One of the simplest and most effective means to nurture, coordinate, and align the three centers is the classical practice known as the Three Treasures Standing Meditation Practice. There are many versions, but my favorite is this one, adapted for you in collaboration with Robert Peng.

⚡ Three Treasures Standing Meditation Practice

The practice consists of five different postures done sequentially:

1. Starting Posture
2. Wisdom Posture
3. Vitality Posture
4. Love Posture
5. Universal Posture

1. Starting Posture

The Starting Posture is the same as the basic standing posture in the Simple Standing Meditation, except your feet may be wider apart—one and a half to two shoulder widths. The right distance varies depending on your weight and body type, so find a position that feels natural to you.

Close your eyes and maintain the Starting Posture for one to three minutes.

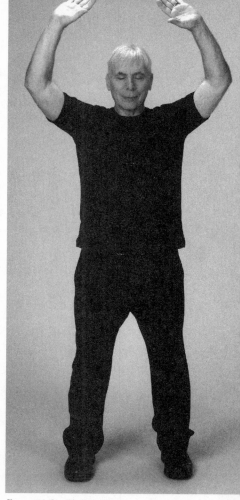

figure 1.3 Three Treasures Standing Meditation, the Wisdom Posture

2. Wisdom Posture

With your eyes still closed, raise your arms slowly to form an open circle above your head. Keep your palms facing upward and outward; the backs of your hands are facing toward your head (figure 1.3). Find a comfortable position that minimizes the tension in your shoulders and arms.

Inhale slowly and deeply, and concentrate the qi in a sphere in the midpoint of your upper center. As you exhale, expand the circumference of your upper center until it fills all the space between your head and your arms, forming a large ball of white light. Feel the essence of your wisdom flowing inside the ball between your hands.

With your palms still facing out, absorb inspiring qi from the heavens through both your palms and your arms. Feel the celestial energy flow into the sphere of your expanded upper center. As you hold this position, relax and become aware of the qi empowering your mind, infusing it with creative inspiration.

Stand in the Wisdom Posture for one to three minutes.

3. Vitality Posture

With your eyes still closed, lower your arms gently and slowly, turning your palms inward, to form an open circle in front of your abdomen (figure 1.4). Imagine that your feet are roots sinking deep into the ground.

figure 1.4   Three Treasures Standing Meditation, the Vitality Posture

Inhale slowly and deeply, and concentrate the qi in a sphere in the midpoint of your lower center. As you exhale, expand your lower center until it fills all the space between your arms, forming a large ball of white light. Feel the essence of vitality flowing inside the ball between your hands.

Now absorb the energy of the earth through your Bubbling Spring points. Allow this nurturing, grounding energy to flow into your expanded lower center. As you hold this position, relax and become aware that you are being nourished by the energy of the earth, the same energy that causes trees to grow and flowers to blossom. This energy is empowering your lower center and infusing it with charisma and the willpower you need to implement your creative ideas.

Stand in the Vitality Posture for one to three minutes.

4. Love Posture

With your eyes still closed, raise your arms slowly and gently to form an open circle in front of your chest. Keep your palms facing your body (figure 1.5). Imagine that you are hugging the horizon.

Inhale slowly and deeply, and concentrate the qi in a sphere in the midpoint of your middle center. As you exhale, expand the circumference of your middle center until it fills all the space between your chest and your

figure 1.5 Three Treasures Standing Meditation, the Love Posture

arms, forming a large ball of white light. Feel the essence of compassion flowing inside the ball between your hands.

Now absorb all the love and tenderness stored in the hearts of all living beings into your middle center. Feel this energy flowing into your expanded middle center. As you hold this position, relax and become aware of the energy of love, infusing your being with compassion and kindness. This energy supports your ability to work creatively with others to realize your creative dreams.

Stand in the Love Posture for one to three minutes.

5. Universal Posture

With your eyes still closed, place your right hand an inch or so in front of your chest. The hand should be vertical, with your fingers pointing up to the sky. Your right palm is open toward your left side; your thumb is toward your sternum. Place your left hand just underneath your navel, with your palm facing up. (See figure 1.6.)

Inhale slowly and deeply, and concentrate the qi in the core of your central channel. As you exhale, expand your central channel above your head up into the sky and down into the earth below your feet. Feel the three centers, also known as the Three Treasures, blending inside the central core of your being. As you do this, visualize yourself standing inside a large pyramid of white light.

figure 1.6 Three Treasures Standing Meditation, the Universal Posture

As you hold this position, relax and become aware of the alignment between your spirit, your creative purpose, and the energy of wisdom, vitality, and love. Stand in the Universal Posture for one to three minutes.

When you are ready, return to the Starting Posture and nourish your qi.

You'll get the most from this practice if you do all five postures together as a complete set, once a day, for three weeks. For the first week, just do one minute in each posture, and then gradually work your way up to two and then three minutes. After three weeks of regular practice, you can explore focusing on the posture that beckons to you the most. If you feel the need for more inspiration and clarity, then do the Wisdom Posture. If you want to feel more grounded and vital, or if you need to strengthen your resolve to complete a creative project, then practice the Vitality Posture. If you are yearning for more of a sense of connection and empathy, do the Love Posture. The Universal Posture is a wonderful way to experience your alignment with your deepest purpose. Each posture is powerful on its own, and together they serve as one of the most elegant, profound practices I've ever experienced.

Creative Energy Ovals

> Creativity is the natural order of life.
> Life is energy: pure creative energy.
> Julia Cameron, The Artist's Way[44]

This is a simple and powerful way to connect with the natural order of life, with pure creative energy. There are many versions of this exercise, but this practice, taught by Robert Tangora, is the most elegant and complete.

In this practice, you'll integrate your personal qi with the qi around you, thereby becoming more receptive to creative illumination. You can do it as a warm-up before any of the other practices or as a complete practice in itself.

Creative Energy Ovals Practice

You can do this practice sitting, standing, or lying down.

Rest your tongue gently on the palatal junction. Bring your attention to the base of the central channel, at the perineum. As you inhale, imagine drawing qi from the base up through your lower back, behind your spine, to the height of your navel. As you exhale, let it cascade and flow down the front of your body, over the front of your spine, returning to the base. If you like, you can imagine the qi as white or golden phosphorescent light.

You can make a graceful lifting gesture with your hands as you draw the qi up. Begin with your hands resting naturally at your sides. As you inhale, lift your hands, palms facing up, to the level of your navel. Then reverse the gesture as you exhale, allowing your hands to gently roll over and the palms to turn downward as you guide the qi back, returning your hands to the starting position. (You'll make a similar hand movement for each step of this prac-tice except the final one. Adapt the hand movements you make based on the directions for guiding the qi. Experiment to discover the hand motions that give you a sense of the qi flowing harmoni-ously.) Repeat one to seven times.

Next, as you inhale, draw the qi up your back from the base to the point at the middle of your shoulder blades—the back of the middle center. As you exhale, allow the qi to flow down the front returning to the base. Repeat one to seven times.

Next, as you inhale, draw the qi up your back to the Jade Pillow, at the occiput. Exhale and guide the qi down the front of your body back to the base. Repeat one to seven times.

Then, as you inhale, draw the qi up your back to the apex. Exhale and guide the qi down the front, returning to the base. Repeat one to seven times.

Now, as you inhale, draw the qi up your back just under and on the surface of your skin. Starting from the Bubbling Spring points at the soles of your feet, draw the qi up the back of your legs, up the back of the torso, and over the top of the head. As you exhale, let the qi flow down the front surface of your body back to the Bubbling Springs. Repeat one to seven times.

For the next circuit, draw up the qi from beneath your feet and move it up the back of your aura, or energy field, as you inhale. As you exhale, allow it to flow down the front of your aura. The distance between the surface of your skin and the outer edge of your energy field varies from person to person, and it also changes based on a wide range of circumstances. If you imagine the energy rising up behind your body and cascading back down the front at a distance of one or two feet, you'll be in the ballpark. Don't worry if you aren't aware of your aura. In the beginning, just imagine it, and soon you will discover that you can indeed feel your personal energy field beyond the confines of your so-called physical body. Repeat one to seven times.

Finish this practice by inhaling and extending your mind out to eternity in all directions. As you inhale, open your arms wide to the sides, as though you were embracing the entire universe. As you exhale, draw the infinite universal creative energy into your lower center, drawing your hands together to cover your lower center with your left and right palms, respectively. Hold this position as you nourish your qi.

Creators on Qi

Jane Barthelemy

Jane Barthelemy is a contemporary Renaissance woman. An accomplished opera singer, healer, jewelry designer, chef, and author of *Good Morning Paleo* and *Paleo Desserts,* she also holds an MBA from Indiana University. Jane comments on the role that qi plays in her creative work:

We often forget that what we see and hear is a tiny reflection of a much greater energetic world. When I forget to connect to this deeper level, I push and try to make things happen through effort. My progress slows to a crawl, and I often encounter intractable resistance. Then I wake up and remember that I'm not running the universe. I recognize, however, that as a citizen of the universe, it is my right and duty to tune in and *ask* how to harmonize with the creative flow.

So when I wish to create something, I begin by cultivating my qi. I do various practices and meditate deeply. When I'm practicing a qi workout, I feel my cells, molecules, and atoms resonating together in harmony internally and with the energy that surrounds me. When I feel this connection to the harmonious flow of qi, I experience what I call "the real me." I'm not someone's opinion of me or even my fabulous self-created personality.

In that pure state of connection to qi, I create an intention, or a prayer—something like, "If it is in harmony with my highest destiny and aligned with the greatest good, I really want this and this to happen." I ask the universe for assistance with my whole heart. I may repeat it every day, and I aim to stay open to guidance in a selfless way.

Sometimes a new project comes to me in a moment of bliss when I'm doing something totally mundane. I stop, listen, and ask, what's this telling me? In the moment of insight, I see the completed project, whether a new line of jewelry, a book, a recipe, or a recital. I feel how beautiful it will be. I use all my senses and imagine how it will bring joy to others and myself. When I imagine into being something that the universe wants to happen anyway, it's effortless. My work becomes play, and the project happens without stress. This works for anybody and everybody—we should teach it in kindergarten!

The through line of all this is the regular practice of cultivating qi. When I tap into the qi and feel in harmony with it, every action is infused with loving intention. And the side benefit is [that] life becomes a joyous creative dance.[45]

Quickening the Spirit of Invention with Cloud Hands

O it is pleasant, with a heart at ease,
Just after sunset, or by moonlight skies,
To make the shifting clouds be what you please.

Samuel Taylor Coleridge (1772–1834), English Romantic poet[46]

"Quickening the spirit of invention" was the phrase that Leonardo da Vinci used to express the idea of cultivating creativity. One of the cultivation methods he suggested is to watch abstract patterns, such as the movement of clouds in the sky. For thousands of years, adepts in China shared the same insight. They knew that creativity emerges from the interaction of active and receptive forces. Aligning our selves with this harmonious balance of opposites is the secret of harmonious balance in life.

Roger Jahnke, OMD, the chief instructor of the Institute of Integral Qigong and Tai Chi in Santa Barbara, California, explains, "When we stop for a while and watch clouds, we slow down, and begin to appreciate the fundamental forces that support our wellbeing and creativity." He adds, "In the grand tradition of qi cultivation, we combine poetic and inspiring imagery with mind-body practice. In other words, we embody the creative inspiration of the movement of the clouds to experience our essential oneness with the creative power of nature."[47]

Watching clouds drift through the sky has always been one of my favorite forms of meditation for inspiring creativity. I've practiced variations of the Cloud Hands movement for decades. In all the variations, your hands move with the quality of drifting clouds as you gently shift your body from side to side. To get you started, I asked Jahnke, who has a gift for making things as simple as possible, to offer this elegant version. Practicing this movement will, as Jahnke says, "help you to become aware of your unlimited power to create."

⚡ Cloud Hands Practice

figure 1.7 Cloud Hands Practice: weight on left foot

Begin in the basic standing posture (see the beginning of the Simple Standing Meditation).

Slowly allow both hands to float up to shoulder level, elbows bent. Allow the hands to gently lift, so that the palms are facing forward, away from your body.

Drop your right hand slowly and cross it in front of your body at the level of the lower center, so that it moves underneath your left hand. Allow the right palm to gently turn upward as the hand moves. At the same time, allow your left wrist to rotate, so that the left palm faces down. Now both hands are on your left side—left high and right low, with the palms facing one another, as if you were holding a beach ball between them.

Now allow the right hand to float up as the left hands drops, and pass both hands in front of the body. Move the hands gently to the right until your right hand is at shoulder height on your right side, and the left hand is underneath it, at the level of your lower center, with the palms facing one another. Pass both hands in front of your body again, so that your left hand is once again up and your right is below.

Continue alternating sides and allowing the hands to change levels until you find a comfortable rhythm. You'll discover that your hands are describing a lateral figure eight, or infinity symbol, representing your infinite potential to create. Allow the hands to move like clouds passing in the sky.

As your hands flow to the left, with the left hand rising, shift your weight to the left foot, so that about 80 percent of it rests on your left leg, and rotate your torso slightly to the left. (See figure 1.7) Keep your eyes on your left hand until it begins to move downward and to the right.

As your hands flow to the right side, with your right hand rising, shift your weight to your right side, so that about 80 percent of it comes to rest on your right leg, and rotate your torso slightly to the right. (See figure 1.8) Watch the rising right hand with soft eyes.

Continue moving slowly between the left and right positions, just as clouds drift slowly. Keep the soles of your feet in full contact with the floor throughout the movement. Allow your breathing to slow down and become more rhythmic, so that it is in harmony with your movements.

figure 1.8 Cloud Hands Practice: weight on right foot

The Mantra of Creation

Inspiration is a slender river of brightness leaping
from a vast and eternal knowledge.

Sri Aurobindo (1872–1950), Indian sage[48]

Alan Finger is one of the world's great yoga masters. His teachings on
the flow of *prana* (the Sanskrit word for qi) are expressed with natu-
ralness, joy, and grace. Raised in an ashram, Finger knows yoga like
Peyton or Eli Manning know football. I asked him to share the simplest,
most powerful practice for cultivating creative energy.

He responded, "The reason we do yoga postures, and I suppose it's
the same in Chinese qi cultivation, is to purify the subtle energetic
channels in our body so that we can become more receptive to creative
universal energy."[49]

In yoga and Chinese qi cultivation, the central channel, from the
apex to the base, is of primary importance. Finger explains, "The central channel is a silvery thread that is plumb-line center from the top
of the head to the perineum. The apex point is the gate to creative universal intelligence. In yoga it is called Brahmarandhra (*Brahma* means
'pure creative universal energy,' *randhra* means 'gate'). The base point,
known as Muladhara, is the root of your vital energy and your connection to the pure power of Mother Nature."[50] (The Chinese call this
power prenatal qi.)

Finger recommends this simple practice for aligning these energies, referred to by the Chinese as the connection between Heaven and
Earth, and tuning the receptivity of the central channel.

Mantra of Creation Practice

Sit comfortably on a chair or cross-legged on a cushion, as you
prefer. The important point is that your spine is upright. Close
your eyes. Place your hands on either side of your ribcage. When
you inhale, feel your ribs expand upward and outward. When you

exhale, feel the ribs contract. As you feel the ribs expand, notice the way the top of your head lengthens away from the base of the central channel at the perineum. As you exhale, feel the contraction as the lower abdomen draws in.

Once you've got that feeling, block your ears with your thumbs, resting your fingers lightly on the top of your head. Make the sound *sah* as you inhale and the sound *hum* as you exhale. These sounds act as tuning forks for the vibration along the central channel. Listen for the echo of the sound as it reverberates. Inhale *sah* and exhale *hum* for two to three minutes. Then lower your hands and stop making the sounds. Feel how the vibrations continue along your central channel.

Now, as you inhale again, draw a sphere of light, the size of a large pearl, straight down along the central channel from the apex to the base. As you exhale, light from the pearl radiates out from the base into every cell of your being. Watch the radiant light permeate your body for two to three minutes, until you feel that your cells are beginning to glow with light. As your body fills with this glow, allow it to expand out into the space around you. Sit for two more minutes, feeling the suffusion of light around your body in all directions.

Alan Finger explains, "Feel your body as you would like it to feel in the shape you would like it to be. As you do this, you are re-creating yourself into a more vital, loving being and a more creative instrument for your purpose here on Earth."[51]

Creators on Qi

Lorie Dechar

Lorie Dechar is the author of *Five Spirits: Alchemical Acupuncture for Psychological and Spiritual Healing* and a senior clinical supervisor at Tri-State College of Acupuncture in New York. She describes a discovery she made about the creative power of qi:

In my ninth year of practice, I began noticing a fascinating phenomenon. I was drawn to particular [acupuncture] points while working with patients. At first, I doubted what I was feeling. But the feeling persisted and grew and gradually became a recognizable, consistent, and distinct sensation. I began to trust it. It was as if there was a doorway in the skin with a tiny magnet embedded in its frame that drew me toward it. When I needled that point, it felt like I caught a fish! The needles grabbed and the energy moved.

Between what I was feeling at the tips of my fingers and my patients' responses, I realized I had found the junctions of qi. Not only did my patients feel better when I needled the points, so did I. The points are wellsprings of life force that energize me as well as my patients.

I also discovered that when qi flow was enlivened by the treatment, benefits accrued that were beyond what I'd learned to expect in acupuncture school. One of my favorite examples is a young mother of four who wanted desperately to find time to meditate, but inevitably, as soon as she sat down on her meditation cushion, one of her kids would need something. Before the treatment, she was frustrated, desperate, and depressed. I suggested she stop trying to figure it out and simply lie down and receive that treatment.

The next week, when she came in, her face was bright, and her attitude was completely different. What happened? The evening after the treatment it occurred to her to stop trying to practice meditation in the formal ways she had been taught.

"I got it," she said.

"You got what?" I asked.

"I got that I just have to start where I am. I don't care anymore if the house is a mess. I don't need a whole hour with everything quiet. Any time I have a minute, I can center myself and bring attention to my breathing. It doesn't matter if I'm in the bathroom or the closet or in front of the kitchen sink. . . . I can sit on the floor and breathe."

I was bowled over. I sat across from this beautiful, beaming woman who was speaking words of wisdom as if it was the most ordinary thing in the world. Without knowing it, she was paraphrasing the Taoist alchemical text *The Secret of the Golden Flower,* which states, "There's no need to fix the length of time of the meditation; it is only essential to set aside all involvements and sit quietly for a while."

As we harmonize our qi, issues that seem irreconcilable resolve in unexpected ways. This is the creative principle at work. And the best part is that if you practice cultivating your qi, even for a minute here or there, it's like giving yourself an acupuncture treatment every day, so that you can live in greater harmony with your own intuitive wisdom.[52]

Inviting Genius Wisdom

Wendy Palmer is a sixth-degree black belt in aikido, a jazz musician, the author of superb books on the theme of leadership embodiment, and a successful international leadership consultant. She writes, "My experience on the aikido mat, playing jazz, and finding ways to bring creative practices and innovative ideas to leaders worldwide is that an intelligent, self-organizing life force is our greatest ally in creative endeavors. As we open ourselves to this power, we become creative beyond our wildest dreams."[53]

Palmer explains:

The *ki* in *aikido* and the *qi* in *qigong* are one and the same. Whatever we call it, this vivifying capacity is inherent in every thought we think and every move we make. The finest, most perfect, exquisite creative essence is available to us with every breath. Yet most people remain unaware of this gift and go on believing that ego and willpower are the keys to manufacturing achievements and manifesting intentions.

The simplest way I know to activate this creative essence is to open your awareness to it. All geniuses allow themselves to open to insights beyond their rational mind and understanding. You too can tap this universal creativity.[54]

Here is a practice for doing just that—for inviting the inspiration of genius into your body, heart, mind, and spirit now. This practice is particularly helpful when you're struggling with a creative challenge and need help making a breakthrough.

⚡ Inviting Genius Practice

Begin by sitting or lying down. Lengthen your spine, smile, and embrace a sense of grace and dignity. As you inhale, extend your awareness to include your full aura. As you exhale, allow the qi to dance through the spaciousness between the atomic particles of your body.

Then invite the wisdom and creativity of your teachers, mentors, and archetypes to come through you. Ask, "How would _____ (Lao Tzu, Pema Chödrön, Morihei Ueshiba, Marie Curie, Leonardo da Vinci, Elizabeth I—whoever your chosen role model is) engage with this challenge?" Open yourself to be a conduit for creative brilliance.

Wendy Palmer explains, "If you stay with this question despite doubt or self-consciousness, you will have access to an unlimited creative resource, and you will be able to address any creative challenge with boundless energy and inspiration."[55]

Aligning Your Qi with the Da Vinci Principles

> You are not IN the universe, you ARE the universe. . . .
> Ultimately you are not a person, but a focal point where
> the universe is becoming conscious of itself.
>
> Eckhart Tolle[56]

In ancient and medieval European philosophy, adepts believed that the world was composed of the elements of air, fire, earth, and water. In addition to these four basic elements, or essences, they posited a fifth essence *(Quinta Essentia)*. The Quintessence was considered to be the

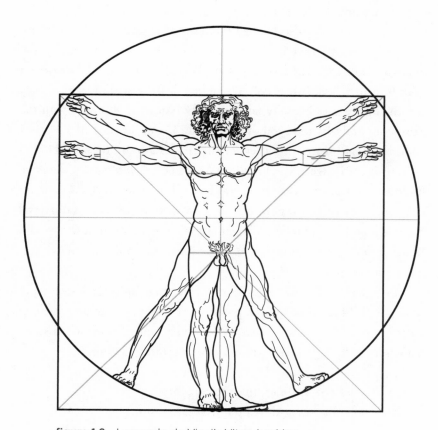

figure 1.9 Leonardo da Vinci's Vitruvian Man

highest element, informing and permeating all of nature and the celestial realm as well. Swiss alchemist Paracelsus (1493–1541) explained, "Man is a microcosm, or a little world, because he is an extract from all the stars and planets of the whole firmament, from the earth and the elements; and so he is their quintessence."[57] Today we use the word *quintessence* to refer to "the most perfect embodiment of something."

The idea that humanity is the most perfect embodiment of creation was reborn in the Renaissance. Leonardo da Vinci's (1452–1519) *Vitruvian Man,* drawn as an illustration for his friend's book on divine proportion, is one of the supreme expressions of this ideal (figure 1.9). Vitruvius (c. 80–15 BCE) was a Roman architect who believed that the human form expressed the principles of universal harmony and that those principles also formed the basis of harmony in architecture. Leonardo himself noted, "Man was called the microcosmos by the ancients, and surely the term was well chosen."[58] The original *Vitruvian Man* is in the collection of the Accademia di Belle Arti in Venice, Italy, but the image is universally familiar and ubiquitous. It appears on the Euro coin and was the symbol for Skylab 3, and it's used as a logo by countless health-care and fitness organizations around the world.

Why is the image of the *Vitruvian Man* so compelling more than five hundred years after the maestro crafted it? The reason is that Leonardo succeeded in representing the human form as an expression of universal harmony, and like all works of great art, it resonates deep in our psyche. In other words, the *Vitruvian Man* reminds us of our oneness with qi, our quintessential integrity.

More than any other figure in history, Leonardo da Vinci represents the fulfillment of human potential. He serves as an archetype of creativity. In *How to Think Like Leonardo da Vinci,* I introduced seven principles to help you learn from history's greatest genius:

1. *Curiosità*—embrace infinite curiosity
2. *Dimostrazione*—develop independent thinking
3. *Sensazione*—sharpen the senses

4. *Sfumato*—embrace ambiguity and change
5. *Arte/Scienza*—integrate logic and imagination
6. *Corporalità*—balance body, mind, and spirit
7. *Connessione*—discover new connections[59]

In this practice, you will embody the principles and align with them energetically so that you may bring them to life in a new way.

Da Vinci Qi Practice

The practice begins with a preparatory attunement followed by seven different movements, one for each principle. Although you will gain maximum benefit by doing them all together in the sequence presented, you needn't feel constrained to do them that way. Each part of the practice can stand alone, so please feel free to do as many as you wish and in the order you like.

Preparation: Embody Divine Proportion

Begin by contemplating Leonardo's *Vitruvian Man* (figure 1.9 on page 49). The image depicts two different arm postures and two different leg postures. Each arm position can be combined with each leg position for a total of four different possible stances. These four body postures are designed to help you access creative universal energy at a high level of vibration. According to Dale Schusterman, DC, author of *Sign Language of the Soul* and my collaborator in developing this preparation step, "When you assume these postures, a deep part of you recognizes a connection with higher frequencies of consciousness, and your nervous system attunes to this new level."[60]

You'll get the most from this preparatory attunement if you maintain a quiet, receptive, witnessing state throughout. Observe yourself observing yourself as you move through the postures.

Refer to the *Vitruvian Man* image as needed as you assume each of the arm and leg positions. In all four positions, you will keep your left foot turned outward and your palms facing forward, the same direction your head is facing. Hold each posture for one full cycle of breath (inhale and exhale), and then proceed to the next one.

1. Start with the legs about twice hip width apart. Your arms are extended out from your shoulders in a horizontal position. Breathe into your lower center.
2. Keep the arms in the horizontal position and bring the left leg in close to the right. Breathe into your lower center.
3. Keep the legs close together and raise your arms slightly above shoulder height. Breathe into your lower center.
4. Keep the arms in the upper position and separate the legs so that they are again about twice hip width apart. Breathe into your lower center.

To finish, simply look at or visualize the image of the *Vitruvian Man.* Place your palms over your center and nourish your qi.

Movement 1. Curiosità—Embrace Infinite Curiosity

Begin in the basic standing posture, facing north. Place your left palm on your lower center, just below your navel, and your right palm on top of the back of your left hand. Breathe naturally.

Gently and gracefully reach your right hand back just behind your right side, stretching it out to the horizon to your right. Follow your hand with your eyes and twist your body slightly so that the movement is easy and natural. Sweep your arm forward as though you are gathering energy and information, and return it to your center. Then gently and gracefully reach your left hand back just behind your left side. Follow your hand with your eyes and twist your body slightly so that the movement is easy and natural. Sweep your hand forward as though you are gathering energy and information, and return it to your center. Then do both hand movements again. This is one cycle. You will do four cycles, one in each of the four directions.

After you complete the first cycle in the north-facing position, step out and around with your left foot so that the toes of your left foot are pointing west. Then gently bring your right foot around so that it's parallel to the left. You are now facing west in the basic standing posture. Repeat the sweeping movements of the hands to the right and then the left, as you did while facing north. Then turn to the south and repeat the pattern. Next, turn to the east and repeat. Finally, return to your original orientation, facing north, with your hands on your lower center.

By looking behind your body, you symbolically demonstrate your openness to new learning. The left and right arm movements together form an infinity symbol, representing your birthright of infinite curiosity. Turning in the four directions reinforces the orientation to explore different perspectives. The two cycles of arm movement in each of the four directions equal a total of eight, and eight again represents infinite curiosity.

Movement 2. Dimostrazione—Develop Independent Thinking
Stand relaxed in a relatively wide stance. Your knees are bent and in alignment with the toes of their respective feet. Place your hands in your hip creases, with the thumbs pointing backwards.

In the first part of this movement, you will be moving your head in a comfortable clockwise circle four times and then in a comfortable counterclockwise circle four times. Begin by gently turning your head to the right, then inhaling as you roll your head down and forward, so your chin comes toward your chest. Exhale as you roll your head up and back to the starting position. Repeat this clockwise circle four times, moving in a gentle, comfortable flow. Then turn your head to the left and repeat the movement four times counterclockwise, making a total set of eight circles.

In the second part of this movement, you will be describing a circle with your torso, first in a clockwise direction four times and then in a counterclockwise direction four times. Rotate your torso in a large circle to the right. Inhale when moving your upper body down and forward. Exhale when moving the upper body back and around to the starting position. Move clockwise four times and then counterclockwise four times.

Keep your mind resting on your lower center throughout this exercise. Dean Y. Deng, MD, who taught me this movement, calls it "throwing away the garbage of the mind." He explains that as you focus on your lower center and make the rotations first of your head and then of your whole torso, you free yourself from attachment to all of your automatic and unenlightened mental habits, thereby liberating your independent thought and nurturing your originality.[61]

Movement 3. Sensazione—Sharpen the Senses

Begin in the basic standing posture. With your eyes closed, begin swinging your arms back and forth in a steady, comfortable rhythm. Keeping the soles of your feet in full contact with the floor, bend both your knees in rhythmic fashion to propel your arms forward and back. As you swing your hands, feel your palms collecting qi like magnets. Be playful and lighthearted as you swing for two minutes.

When you finish swinging, your hands will be pulsating with qi. Bring your palms up just a few inches away from the front of your face. With the palms in this position, move from the shoulders to make a circular motion, as though you were polishing a mirror, seven times in a clockwise direction and then seven times in a counterclockwise direction. Feel the energy radiating from your palms and imagine that it is purifying your senses, literally cleansing the doors of perception. Allow the energy to cleanse your vision, hearing, smell, taste, balance, kinesthesia, and then your inner sight.

When you complete the seven circles in each direction, cup your palms and place them over the orbits of your closed eyes. Enjoy the darkness as you rest and refresh all your senses. Breathe into your lower center. After three cycles of breath, gently remove your hands from your eyes. Open your eyes to look upon the world as though you are seeing it for the first time.

figure 1.10 Leonardo da Vinci's painting of St. John

Movement 4. Sfumato—Embrace Ambiguity and Change

This movement is drawn from Leonardo's mysterious painting of St. John, which resides in the Louvre in Paris. (See figure 1.10.)

Begin in the basic standing posture. Place your left hand on your heart center. Moving from your shoulder, bring your right hand in front of your body, bend your elbow, and point your index finger toward heaven (figure 1.11). (Your palm faces toward your face.) As your hand spirals upward, raise the heel of your right foot, so that you're on the ball of your right foot and your weight shifts onto your left foot. Allow your head to lean a bit to the right. Imitate St. John's mysterious smile. Your eyes glance up to heaven, past the right index fingertip.

Then shift your weight and reverse the posture, so that the right hand caresses your heart center and the left index finger points up to the sky. Smile and glance past the left index finger to heaven above. Repeat six more times on each side, for a total of seven.

This practice strengthens your confusion endurance. As you touch your heart, you empower your emotional intelligence, and as you point to heaven, you invoke the Muse and awaken spiritual intelligence. As the body twists gently, forming an upward-flowing spiral, you wring out anxiety and fear in the face of uncertainty. The toes of the weightless

figure 1.11 The Da Vinci Qi Practice, Movement 4, Sfumato (Embrace Ambiguity and Change)

foot stay energetically connected to the ground as you stretch to the sky, helping you integrate the higher energies that you are summoning in this movement. The glance and smile encourage a delightful nonchalance in the midst of mystery.

Movement 5. Arte/Scienza—Integrate Logic and Imagination

With your eyes closed, step into a wide stance, about two shoulder widths apart. Raise your arms and hands slowly upward, without unduly raising your shoulders, until your arms form an open circle around your upper center (figure 1.12). (This arm position is the same as the Wisdom Posture in the Three Treasures Standing Meditation Practice, except that now your palms are facing toward your head.)

Imagine the light of the sun shining through the back of your right hand into your upper center, and the light of the moon shining through the back of your left hand into your upper center. Feel the bright, yellow, warm light of the sun shining through your right hand, empowering your logical, analytical, and rational mind. Feel the cool, subtle, silvery light of the moon shining through your left hand, empowering your imaginative, nonlinear, intuitive awareness. Enjoy this practice for three to seven cycles of breath.

figure 1.12 The Da Vinci Qi Practice, Movement 5, Arte/Scienza (Integrate Logic and Imagination)

Movement 6. Corporalità—Balance Body, Mind, and Spirit

Begin in a wide version of the basic standing posture, with your feet approximately double shoulder width apart. Then, maintaining the length of your spine, slowly fold your hip creases and bend your knees, resulting in a comfortable squat. As you move into the squat, bring your hands down and around in front of your body, as though you are gathering qi up from the earth. At the bottom of the squat, your wrists cross. (See figure 1.13.)

Now rise back up to standing by pushing down through your Bubbling Spring points, unfolding the hip creases, and straightening the knees, without locking them. Keep your tailbone releasing downward, even as your legs straighten and your torso rises. As you rise, keep your wrists crossed and allow your hands to float up the center of the body. As your wrists reach the level of your middle center, allow them to begin separating. At the top of the movement, your hearts of the palms are facing away from your head, as though you were gathering qi from the sky (figure 1.14).

Slowly squat again, bringing your arms down to gather the earth qi, then crossing the wrists at the bottom of the movement. Then repeat the upward movement. Continue squatting and folding the arms down and in and then rising and allowing the arms to unfold. Do seven complete cycles.

figure 1.13 The Da Vinci Qi Practice, Movement 6, Corporalità (Balance Body, Mind, and Spirit)

After a little practice, you'll discover that your arms are describing two intersecting circles as you move up and down. You'll get the most benefit if you can coordinate the arm and body movements so that at the bottom of the squat the arms are at their lowest point and at the top the arms are at their highest. As you squat down, you are compressing all the joints and even the cells of your body, consolidating the qi in the core of your being. As you open out like a blossoming flower, you allow the qi to expand through every cell and all your joints. This harmonious pulsing of your whole being brings your body, mind, and spirit into balance.

Movement 7. Connessione— Discover New Connections

Begin in the basic standing posture. Close your eyes and bring your hands into prayer position in front of your chest; touch your thumbs to your chest. Feel blessed as your middle center expands with love and gratitude.

From this prayer position, lower your hands down past your lower center, allowing your palms

figure 1.14 The Da Vinci Qi Practice, Movement 6, Corporalità (Balance Body, Mind, and Spirit)

to move apart as you do. Slowly raise your arms out to your sides so that they are extended horizontally from your shoulders, parallel with the ground, palms facing the earth. Absorb the energy of the earth through your hearts of the palms.

Use a gentle but complete undulation of your whole body from your Bubbling Spring points to your apex to rotate your palms until they turn upward, toward the sky. As you do this simple movement, feel that you are standing at the center of the universe, flipping the elemental forces of creation. Feel the tidal force of spiraling galaxies swirling around as you rotate your arms.

With this sense of infinite power, raise your arms over your head, palms facing inward, and gather qi. Then guide the qi down through your apex and central channel by bringing your hands down the centerline in front of your body, with your palms facing down. Feel the rush as the energy follows your hands down the central channel like a pillar of brilliant light.

When your hands and the light reach your lower center, place your palms on your abdomen. Slide your palms down your inner thighs and down the insides of your legs. Then slide your palms over the tops of your feet and outward, around to the back of your ankles. Begin to slide them up around your heels and calves. Continue to draw your palms up the back of your legs, over your buttocks to your lower back and upward to your kidney area, all the way up toward your shoulder blades. Then return your hands to prayer position in front of your middle center.

Rest for a moment. Allow the qi you've collected to fill you with a sense of connectedness to the whole universe. Smile and feel blessed. Repeat this movement sequence three to seven times.

End the Da Vinci Qi Practice by placing your hands over your lower center, with one hand on top of the other, and nourishing your qi.

Creators on Qi

Kaleo and Elise Ching

Kaleo and Elise Ching practice qi cultivation as the basis of their work as authors, artists, teachers, and healers. Qi is also a catalyst for their relationship. As Kaleo explains, "Our first date in 1988 was to tai chi class, so we have a long history of qi awareness together."[62]

Kaleo and Elise practice qi cultivation together, and they've noticed how the practice supports the deepening of their relationship and their creative collaboration. The energetic harmony they discovered in their own relationship led them to originate and co-teach classes in qi cultivation, so others can experience the empowering effect on their creative expression.

Kaleo also offers individual healing sessions designed to help his clients experience the sense of wholeness that emerges when the natural flow of qi is restored. He comments on the relationship between his healing work and his art:

> As a practitioner combining various healing modalities, I love how qi informs the work. Qi cultivation has taught me how to ground, center, and generate an abundance of energy to share. When I work as an artist, gratitude flows in being able to channel qi into painting on canvas or sculpting with clay. Painting and sculpting, massage and energy healing work, are creative art forms. Layering paint on canvas is like working textures and layers of the body in massage. Spreading colors on canvas is like adjusting the body's vibrations or like balancing heat or cold, or deficient or excessive energetic patterns. Sculpting clay is like kneading muscles and invigorating tendons along the bones. Laying gauze on a person's face or body to make a mask mold is like stretching and smoothing fascia. Pulling the mask away from the skin after it's dried is like lifting

and cleansing energetic psycho-emotional layers after a massage or energy healing session.[63]

Q and A   Mastering Creative Energy

Q *How does qi cultivation affect health and wellness?*

A "If you want to be healthy and live to 100, do qigong."[64] That's what Mehmet Oz, MD, told Oprah Winfrey and millions of others. For thousands of years, people practicing qi cultivation have experienced profound health benefits. Contemporary research shows that this approach to "meditation in motion" also functions, as described in an article in the newsletter of Harvard Medical School, as "medication in motion."[65]

In addition to teaching tai chi and qigong, Roger Jahnke is a doctor of Oriental Medicine and the author of *The Healing Promise of Qi: Creating Extraordinary Wellness Through Qigong and Tai Chi.* In a meta-study entitled "A Comprehensive Review of Health Benefits of Qigong and Tai Chi" in the *American Journal of Health Promotion,* Jahnke et al. concluded that qi cultivation (the researchers treated tai chi and qigong as effectively the same) results in measurable benefits related to "bone health, cardiopulmonary fitness, physical function, falls prevention and balance, general quality of life . . . immunity, and psychological factors such as anxiety, depression and self-efficacy."[66]

Jahnke offers a four-point manifesto for understanding the revolutionary possibilities of qi cultivation for healing and wellness:

1. **The most profound medicine is produced within the human body for free.** The most perfect pharmaceuticals aren't produced by big drug companies, but rather by your own system. Qi-cultivation practices are designed to optimize your natural healing biochemistry.

2. **This medicine based on qi cultivation is now universally accessible.** The traditional approach held the power of qi under wraps; it was brokered by a clannish lineage system. As Jahnke emphasizes, "Democratization of qi is founded in the Jeffersonian ideal of inalienable rights—not just liberty from political tyranny or misinformation, but also liberation from internal constraints and false assumptions."

3. **Maximize the righteous qi.** In the West we try to find the pathogenic factor or process and eradicate or retard it. This is occasionally necessary. Jahnke advocates another ideal: "Rather than trying to figure out what is wrong and trying to stop it, focus on maximizing what is right to increase and extend it." In Chinese medicine this is called maximizing the righteous qi.

4. **Guard the One.** Health and freedom exist in direct association with a connection to a spiritual source. When we cultivate our connection to that source, "the One," we tap an aspect of our being that is eternally well. As Jahnke explains, "Qi cultivation allows us to connect experientially with the eternal self in limited time."[67]

Qi cultivation strengthens your vitality, and enhanced vitality is a key to liberating creativity. As Jahnke explains, "The average human being has a longing to create but is not necessarily well enough, or energized enough, to fulfill it. For many people, qi cultivation provides a missing link in their quest to realize their creative potential." He adds, "With greater vitality we are able to think, feel, and act more creatively. And these practices awaken the aspect of our self that is completely unlimited and free of influence from any bias or preconception—the eternal self or spirit—thus summoning the transcendental energy of higher creativity."[68]

Q *Isn't all this just a form of the placebo effect?*

A Maybe. As humorist Steven Wright says, "I'm addicted to placebos. I tried to quit, but I can't tell if I have or not."

Whether the results of qi cultivation are placebo effects or not, they have consistently helped people to feel better and raise their creative energy for thousands of years.

Q *Is there any scientific evidence for qi?*

A William A. Tiller, PhD, is a fellow of the American Academy for the Advancement of Science and professor emeritus at Stanford University's department of Materials Science and Engineering. He is a pioneer in the scientific study of consciousness. He writes, "For the last four hundred years, an unstated assumption of science is that human intention cannot affect what we call 'physical reality.' Our experimental research of the past decade shows that . . . this assumption is no longer correct."[69]

Tiller's research illuminates the ways in which our intention affects our subtler energies—in other words, our qi. Tiller explains that qi "appears to function in the empty space between the fundamental electric particles. . . . As such, it is currently invisible to us and to our traditional measurement instruments."[70] He and his colleagues have devised ingenious methods to measure the effect of intention on, for example, the acid-alkaline balance of water. Their results are consistent and replicable. Tiller summarizes, "The substance in this new level is influenced by human intention."[71]

Science is just at the beginning of understanding these subtler phenomena, but the human technology for working with this energy has evolved over thousands of years so that we can raise our level of wellness and creativity now. Tiller emphasizes, "We humans are much more than we think we are." And the key to the fulfillment of our exceptional potential is the "conscious application of inner self management techniques like . . . qigong."[72]

Q   *Is qi ever visible?*

A   Some people see the flow of qi both through the body and in the atmosphere. If you practice qi cultivation regularly, you may see the light. Emily Dickinson described it as *phosphorescence;* she refers to it as the "light within" and "the genius behind poetry."[73]

Q   *How do I know if I'm feeling qi moving in my body?*

A   People experience the flow of qi in different ways. Sometimes it manifests as warmth or as a pleasant feeling of fullness, especially in the hands. It can also feel like an electromagnetic tingling or a pleasurable version of pins and needles. After more concentrated practice, you may experience a sense of energetic streaming, like a gushing flow of water pulsing through the spine and limbs.

   Some people feel distinct sensations of qi flowing as soon as they start to practice qi cultivation, while others don't feel much at first. You needn't worry about trying to feel the qi. If you practice with an open, positive attitude, you will get the benefits, whatever your level of sensitivity.

Q   *What's the difference between qigong and tai chi?*

A   Qigong, the art of cultivating qi, is the source of tai chi, and tai chi is effectively a complex qigong practice. Qi cultivation is the wellspring of many of the extraordinary treasures of Chinese culture, which also include traditional Chinese medicine (TCM), feng shui, and various other martial arts, such as kung fu.

   In Chinese medicine, illness is conceived as the result of impediments to the flow of qi, and various therapies, such as acupuncture, are designed to restore the harmonious flow. Feng shui is more than just an approach to interior and landscape design; it's a system for facilitating the harmonious flow of qi in a living environment. Kung fu and other martial arts are all predicated on qi cultivation; that's the source of the power. Tai chi originated as a martial art in Chen Village, China, and later became the preferred martial practice of the palace guards of the emperor. Although it is mostly practiced today for its health benefits, you'll discover that the health benefits are greater if you understand the martial applications of the movements.

Q *How do I find a good teacher of qigong or tai chi?*

A You can start by checking out the teachers referenced in the text. Websites and other relevant information are available in the "Recommended Resources" section. And there are many other excellent teachers besides the ones I've interviewed for this book.

Good teachers in all disciplines create positive learning environments and aim to empower their students. Qi is power, and power can corrupt unless the teacher is open and responsive to feedback. Kung fu legend Bruce Lee (1940–1973) said, "A good teacher protects his pupils from his own influence."[74]

The notion that you are your own best teacher sounds like a spiritual-path cliché, but it is true. An external teacher's job is to share inspiration, provide technical details, and reflect your true nature.

You can learn a lot by practicing the material in these pages, and get a taste of the teachings of various masters. You can buy the books or order the CDs and DVDs of the teachers introduced here in order to learn more.

It is wonderful to attend live classes or seminars in qi cultivation with a master teacher. A master's brainwaves resonate at high-amplitude alpha waves and secondary theta waves while he is sending healing energy to subjects, according to a study conducted at The Menninger Clinic.[75] The subjects' brainwaves soon resonate with the identical pattern, which is associated with relaxation, healing, and creative insight. I believe that something similar happens in a class with an experienced teacher: when you practice qi cultivation with a master teacher, it's easier to feel the qi.

Although I've experienced a direct transmission of amazingly powerful qi from many gifted masters, I find that the greatest benefits accrue from my own daily practice.

Q *There are many practices described here. How do I decide which ones are best for me?*

A All of these practices are designed to help you enhance your creativity. After you read through them, you may feel drawn to experiment with the one that beckons to you the most. If you don't have a clear intuition as to a particular practice, then simply experiment with one for a few days and then move on to another. After you go through them all, you will discover the ones that inspire you the most.

Q *Once I decide on the practices that appeal to me most, what's the best way to proceed?*

A Do the practice or practices that appeal to you most every day if you can. And if you can, do them consistently at a particular time of day to help you get in a rhythm. For example, let's say you are drawn to the Three Treasures Standing Meditation Practice. You may decide to do it each morning or during your lunch break or right after work.

Once you decide on a practice, it's a good idea to do it every day for three weeks. After three weeks, you can switch to another practice or continue with the one you like most. If you have more than twenty minutes per day, you may do multiple practices each day. It's best to continue with one core practice and then, when you have more time, experiment with another.

Q *What if I don't have twenty minutes to do a practice each day?*

A Some of the practices, such as the Da Vinci Qi Practice and the Three Treasures Standing Meditation Practice, require up to twenty minutes, while others, such as the Creative Energy Ovals Practice, can be completed in less than five minutes. If you are pressed for time, then simply do one of the shorter exercises.

Q *You write that it's OK to do these practices anytime, but aren't some times better than others?*

A In traditional practice qi cultivation is coordinated with the different energies of different times of day and with the cycles of the moon and other seasonal influences. When you practice in harmony with the shifting energies of the external world, you may experience an exquisite sense of harmony with nature and the universe. Given the unnatural circumstances that predominate in contemporary life, I've chosen practices designed to provide optimal benefits at any time. (It's best not to practice immediately after a big meal simply because your qi is drawn by the digestive process and isn't as available.) If you practice consistently for just twenty minutes each day, you'll soon discover that your sensitivity to the flow of energy, through the day and through the seasons, becomes much more acute.

Q *Is it better to practice in a beautiful place, like out in a garden or in a room with refined feng shui?*

A It's a special pleasure to practice qi cultivation in beautiful places. I've enjoyed these practices on some of the most beautiful beaches of the world, underneath the Oculus of the Pantheon in Rome, on a private courtyard overlooking the Taj Mahal, and on the Acropolis in Greece, to name just a few. In those exquisite settings qi is readily available, so I felt uplifted and energized just by being there. The real beauty and power of these practices is that they can transform an airport lounge, a generic hotel room, or a parking lot behind a Chuck E. Cheese into a Shangri-la.

Q *Is it beneficial to practice in a group?*

A Practicing in a group offers many benefits. In addition to providing social bonding, group practice also seems to magnify the effects of the exercises. Practitioners refer to this as the creation of a qi field. When we enliven our qi, we tend to feel more connected to the energy around us, so it makes sense that when we practice together, we can experience an enhanced sense of energy and connection.

On the other hand, all the exercises can be enjoyed solo. You don't need to go to a class or find a partner to practice.

Q *What's the most important element in the practices?*

A Practice is the most important element of practice. In other words, "Just do it." Filmmaker Woody Allen said, "Eighty percent of success is just showing up."[76] If you show up and practice every day, you will be transformed. And when you practice, the most important element is your attitude. If you bring a creative mindset and embrace your practice with gratitude, you will multiply the benefits.

Q *Could you give an example of how you apply these practices yourself?*

A Qi cultivation is one of the keys to my creativity, stamina, and well-being, especially when I'm on the road. On a recent trip to Australia, for example, I gave four full-day seminars and two keynotes in three different cities in a period of ten days. Then I boarded a twenty-three-hour flight from Sydney to London. We stopped over in Singapore. I found a quiet corner of the transfer lounge and did the Creative Energy Ovals Practice and the Three Treasures Standing Meditation Practice. When we landed in London, there was a long line at Immigration, so I did a combination of the Simple Standing Meditation and Simple Qi Walking Practice (when the queue finally moved).

The result: less jet lag and a greater sense of vitality and peace. After two days in London visiting friends, I flew to Basel to give a keynote and workshop at the Swiss Innovation Forum. I did the Da Vinci Qi Practice before my talk and wasn't surprised when a participant asked afterward, "You must have given this presentation thousands of times, right? But your energy and enthusiasm was amazing! How do you do that?" In essence my answer was, "It's not me. It's the qi."

PART 2

MASTERING *the* CREATIVE MINDSET

Creativity is not a talent. It is a way of operating.

John Cleese, British actor[1]

Creativity Self-Assessment

Let's set the stage for our exploration of the creative mindset by assessing your attitude toward your own creative abilities.

How Creative Are You?

Please reflect on the following statements and note which ones feel most accurate for you now.

- I don't have a creative cell in my body.
- I am not very creative.
- My (brother, sister, etc.) was the creative one in our family, not me.
- I am about average in my creative ability.
- I'm creative outside of my workplace.
- Creativity is just for artists, and artists are crazy and dysfunctional.

- I was creative when I was much younger, but I've lost touch with that part of myself.
- I'm a little bit more creative than average.
- I am considerably more creative than average.
- I'm a creative genius.

Your reflection on these statements will help you assess your sense of confidence in your creative ability. Perhaps you believe you are creative in some areas of your life but not in others. Maybe, like many of my clients, you don't think you're very creative, but you have a glimmer of hope that you might learn how to be more so. Or perhaps you are confident in your creative ability but want to know how to develop it further.

How Creative Can You Become?

Please reflect on the following statements and note your responses. Do you agree or disagree?

- People are born with a certain amount of creative ability, and it's unlikely that they can change it.
- Creativity is a matter of talent. You either have it or you don't.
- Creativity isn't something that can be taught.
- It may be possible to improve creativity a little.
- Although individuals may be born with different degrees of talent, they can, with appropriate training, become more creative.
- Creative thinking is a skill that can be learned and developed throughout life.
- People who believe they are not creative can change and become very creative.

This second set of statements will help you reflect on your current mindset about creativity. If you are more in agreement with the first three statements, then your mindset is probably limiting your ability. In the pages that follow, you will learn how to change that mindset. If you are more in agreement with the last four statements, then you are already on your way, and you will learn how to refine and develop your creative powers.

Embrace a Creative Mindset

Q: How many qigong masters does it take to change a light bulb? A: Only one, but the light bulb has to have a creative mindset.

Growing up in New Jersey, I didn't know that it was possible to learn things without having a talent for them. I was sure that I would never, for example, learn to sing, draw, or swim. I believed that creativity was something you either had or not, and I developed a more enlightened approach, very slowly, over many years.

You are about to learn how to accelerate the process of this enlightenment. *The creative mindset* is my term for the attitudes and orientations that optimize creativity. These include playfulness, a sense of purpose, chutzpah, courage, persistence in the face of uncertainty, an appreciation for beauty and nature, and a deep humility that is the soul of creative confidence.

A mindset, according to *The American Heritage Dictionary,* is "a habitual or characteristic mental attitude that determines how you will interpret and respond to situations." Mindset functions all the time, for better or for worse, whether we are conscious of it or not. It serves as a filter for our experience and it has a powerful influence on every aspect of our lives. Psychologists have known for many years that mindsets have a huge influence on our moods, our perceptual abilities, and our general level of happiness. And mindset is probably the most important influence on our creative ability.

Our thoughts, feelings, energy, and physiology always work together and can't really be separated. Our language reflects our bias to artificially disconnecting these aspects of ourselves. Although mindset tends to be thought of as primarily mental, when used here it also refers to an emotional and a physical/energetic state.

Stanford University psychologist Carol S. Dweck, PhD, has conducted research on the effects of mindset on achievement and success in many areas of life. Her work confirms that mindset makes a tremendous difference in our performance on many levels. Dweck elucidates two major mindsets: the *fixed mindset* and the *growth mindset.*[2]

People with a fixed mindset believe that fundamental abilities like creativity, intelligence, or coordination are predetermined and unchangeable. A fixed mindset leads people to defend their status quo, avoid feedback, and fear mistakes. People with a fixed mindset believe that talent alone is the key to success.

Those with a growth mindset, on the other hand, believe that fundamental abilities like creativity, intelligence, or coordination can be developed and improved throughout life. Whatever their talent level, they believe that effort, perseverance, and practice are the keys to excellence. Because of their dedication to improvement, they are not afraid of feedback or of making mistakes. People with a growth mindset are more resilient and more committed to lifelong learning.

Dweck's research also demonstrates that people with a fixed mindset can change, and people who already have a growth mindset can strengthen and refine it to generate even better results in their chosen endeavors. Some people are clearly born with more talent than others; we don't all start with the same gifts in music, mathematics, or sports, for example. But Dweck's research shows conclusively that in the long run the growth mindset trumps talent, and the fixed mindset limits the fulfillment of talent.

We have a choice about the attitudes we adopt, and these attitudes have a profound influence on our lives. We can choose to shift from a fixed to a growth mindset, which is the first essential key to the creative mindset. The four-step process of changing begins with self-observation.

Step 1: Observe the Voice of Your Fixed Mindset

When you are considering a creative challenge—preparing a presentation; trying to generate a new product idea or marketing strategy;

making up a new recipe; beginning to write an article, poem, song, or book—listen for the internal voice of the fixed mindset. It says things like, "This requires creative talent that I don't have," "I'll never be any good at this," and, "I'm not creative enough."

If, despite the negative promptings of this internal voice, you manage to start your endeavor, you may find that the voice becomes even shriller when you experience a difficulty or setback. In the face of adversity, the voice of the fixed mindset says things like, "This is hard because I'm not creative," "I knew that I wasn't cut out for this!" and, "This requires creative abilities that I just don't have."

For the fixed mindset, it's hard to start a creative project, and even harder to persevere through adversity, but it gets even worse when exposed to criticism or negative feedback.

Facing criticism, the fixed mindset says things like, "When I try to be creative, I immediately get shot down," "Why are they focusing on only what's wrong?" and, "This negative feedback confirms my lack of creativity."

People with a fixed mindset tend to interpret even carefully presented constructive feedback as a form of attack. The core message they hear is, "You're not good enough. And you never will be good enough." Moreover, the fixed mindset doesn't have to wait for external critical feedback. It's devastatingly self-critical.

As you start to pay attention to the voice of the fixed mindset, do your best to observe it without judgment. Notice what it says and the tone with which it speaks. Bring your awareness to the state of your body, energy, and breathing when it speaks. You'll probably notice that it's associated with an interference with breathing or qi flow and that you tend to contract your body into a more fixed state when it's speaking.

Step 2: Choose How to Interpret a Situation

Humans differ from other animals by the broader scope of our potential responses to a stimulus. In other words, we have the power to choose many of our attitudes and actions. You can apply this power to the way you approach creative challenges and to the way you interpret mistakes, difficulties, or criticism.

You are free to choose a fixed mindset that emphasizes your lack of talent or ability. As Homer Simpson, master of the fixed mindset, counsels, "You tried your best and you failed miserably. The lesson is, never try." Simpson explains, "If something is too hard to do, then it's not worth doing. You just stick that guitar in the closet next to your shortwave radio, your karate outfit, and your unicycle, and we'll go inside and watch TV."[3]

Or you can consciously embrace a growth mindset, and reframe difficulties and challenges as learning opportunities. In the words of another Homer, the Greek epic poet (eighth century BCE) who wrote *The Iliad* and *The Odyssey,* "And what he greatly thought, he nobly dared."[4] Dare to commit to growth and choose to view feedback, even feedback that is less than constructive, as fuel for your quest to improve.

This commitment is especially important when you are beginning in a creative endeavor, because you may experience a wide gap between your taste and abilities. In other words, people with refined taste may be even more discerning of the weaknesses of their current abilities, thus making it difficult for them to persevere. A growth mindset is, therefore, especially important for the person with refined sensibilities.

Ira Glass, the host of National Public Radio's *This American Life,* is a master storyteller renowned for his insightful, creative, and engaging broadcasts. He explains, "We do creative work, and we get into it because we have good taste . . . [B]ut it's like there's a gap . . . [F]or the first couple years that you're making stuff, what you're making is not that great, . . . but your taste is killer . . . [Y]our taste is good enough that you can tell that what you're making is kind of a disappointment." Glass adds that many people never get past this phase. He emphasizes that the people he knows who do interesting creative work all went through this phase for years until the quality of their work caught up with their discernment. He adds, "In my case I took longer to figure out how to do this than anybody I ever met."[5]

Step 3: Answer the Voice of Your Fixed Mindset with the Voice of Your Growth Mindset

People with a fixed mindset tend to resist feedback and opportunities to change and grow partly because they are self-critical in a way that isn't constructive. As they grow up, they internalize the voices of their most judgmental, negative teachers, bosses, or relatives. This internalized self-criticism makes it too painful to risk the mistakes and awkwardness that inevitably characterize the attempt to be creative.

The voice of the fixed mindset is often harshly self-demeaning. The voice of the creative mindset is self-compassionate and encouraging. In a study entitled "Don't Be So Hard on Yourself: Self-Compassion Facilitates Creative Originality Among Self-Judgmental Individuals," psychologists Darya L. Zabelina and Michael D. Robinson found that changing the internal dialogue from one that focuses on self-criticism to one that is compassionate tends to result in higher scores on creativity tests. They noted that self-critical tendencies "may undermine creative expressions among certain individuals." And they discovered that "[a] self-compassionate mindset may facilitate higher levels of creative originality."[6]

Let's say, for example as you approach a creative challenge, that the fixed mindset says, "This requires creative talent that I don't have. I'll never be any good at this."

The growth mindset answers, "I'm not certain, but if I apply myself I can probably find a way."

Fixed mindset: "But what happens if I fail? It will be a disaster!"

Growth mindset: "It's only a failure if I give up. If my first effort fails, I will learn from that and find a way to improve."

Fixed mindset: "This is too risky. I feel uncomfortable."

Growth mindset: "Nothing creative is ever accomplished without risk. On my deathbed I'm more likely to regret never trying than trying and dealing with discomfort."

When you encounter adversity, the fixed mindset might tell you, "This is hard because I'm not creative. If I were gifted in this area, I wouldn't be having so much trouble."

You can use your growth mindset to reply, "The assumption that things always come easy to those with talent is false. Jefferson, Curie, and Edison all made huge mistakes but never stopped learning and improving. Even Leonardo da Vinci, the most talented person who ever lived, had to overcome major faux pas. Leonardo wrote notes of encouragement to himself in the margins of his notebooks—'Obstacles cannot crush me' and 'Every obstacle yields to stern resolve.'"[7]

As you face criticism, you might hear your fixed mindset say, "This criticism confirms my lack of creative talent."

You can counter it with your growth mindset: "This feels painful, but I know that feedback is just data. What can I learn from what I've just heard? Is there a way it could help me improve? Even if most of it is off the mark, is there anything I can use to help me get better?"

Step 4: Take the Action That Is Based on the Growth Mindset

As you practice a mindful internal dialogue, you'll discover that it's possible to experience the doubts and fears associated with the fixed mindset, but that they needn't constrain your choice to guide your actions by the growth mindset.

As Dweck emphasizes, almost everyone who accomplishes something great overcomes doubt and fear through persistence and commitment. She cites Mozart, Darwin, and Michael Jordan, among many others, as exemplars of the growth mindset.

As you adopt a growth mindset and deliberately practice the methods that you will learn in the following pages, you will be moving toward the realization of your creative dreams.

Qi Cultivation to Shift from a Fixed Mindset to a Creative Mindset

All of the qi-cultivation exercises in this book will help support your shift from a fixed mindset to a more creative growth mindset. The first movement of the Da Vinci Qi Practice, *Curiosità* (page 52), is particularly helpful in this regard. Additionally, you may want to explore the following practice, which is designed especially to ignite and sustain your creative fire and free you from habits and blocks associated with the fixed mindset.

⚡ Ignite and Sustain the Fire of Genius

This practice is best done in a quiet place, where you will be free from distractions. The first time you do this, do all three steps in sequence. Later you can do any single step of the practice on its own, as the spirit moves you.

Step 1. Sit on a chair at a table. Place a lighted candle on the table a few feet from you.

Sit upright and begin following the flow of your breathing in the manner introduced in the Embryonic Breathing Meditation: Breathe slowly and deeply, allowing your belly to expand as you inhale. Bring extra attention to the moments when your inhalation shifts to an exhalation and when your exhalation shifts to inhalation.

Contemplate the movement of the flame for a minute or two.

Step 2. As you inhale, imagine that you're drawing the essence of the light and warmth from the flame into your lower center. Envision the flame shining within your lower center. Allow this fire in your

figure 2.1 In step 3 of Ignite and Sustain the Fire of Genius, first the hands form the shape of a flame in front of the heart. Then the arms sweep overhead to form a second flame shape.

belly to illuminate your vitality. Contemplate the inner flame of vitality for one minute.

Now picture your individual thoughts, worries, and fears associated with a fixed mindset as dry autumn leaves. Allow each individual leaf to float down from your mind and drop into the fire in your belly. As the lower-center fire ignites each leaf, watch it burn and be converted into energy that fuels your enthusiasm for learning, change, and creativity. Practice this meditation for up to five minutes.

Step 3. Stand up and spread your feet about double shoulder width apart. Move your hands into a prayer position at your heart. Allow your body to soften and sink down a little as your arms sweep back behind your torso and then float forward in front of your body, so that they are comfortably extended at the height of your chest. Bring your middle fingertips together with your palms facing outward, so that your hands make the shape of a flame (figure 2.1). Then draw your hands back into the prayer position at your middle center.

Now gently stretch your arms straight out horizontally from your shoulders, so your body

figure 2.2 In step 3 of Ignite and Sustain the Fire of Genius, first the hands form the shape of a flame in front of the heart. Then the arms sweep overhead to form a second flame shape.

makes a T shape. As your arms reach full extension, sweep them up overhead to make the shape of a flame vertically, with your middle fingertips touching above the head, palms facing inward (figure 2.2). As the fingertips touch, gently draw the hands down in front of you, back to the prayer position at your middle center.

As you make the flame shapes and then draw the hands back to your heart, you are fueling your fire of genius so that you can sustain it in the face of difficulty. One horizontal plus one vertical flame movement constitutes one repetition. Perform eight repetitions and then finish by nourishing your qi.

Creators on Qi

Kaleo and Elise Ching

In addition to their individual therapeutic work, art, and public seminars, Kaleo and Elise Ching also teach qi cultivation to people in challenging circumstances, such as inmates in a psychiatric unit of a county jail and veterans suffering from post-traumatic stress disorder (PTSD). In situations such as these, most people are locked into a limiting fixed mindset about their potential on many levels. Qi practices can have a profoundly transformational effect.

"In environments like these, where people are wounded and traumatized, words don't necessarily have much weight, but the quality of energy and intention does," Kaleo and Elise explain. "First we aim to create an atmosphere of safety and nonjudgment with a sense of appreciation for each person's gifts."[8]

Kaleo, Elise, and I agree that when students feel recognized and accepted for who they are and then encouraged to express themselves, whether in a corporate environment, a prison, or a hospital, they blossom. Kaleo comments on his work in the jail psychiatric unit: "Inmates discovered an unfamiliar sense of inner peace as they did qi-cultivation meditations and worked on their art and masks." The masks were good enough that Kaleo was able to sell them and then put the proceeds into the prisoner's commissary fund, so that the inmates could buy sundries or snacks. He says, "They always asked me to spend some of the money to have a celebration, with fresh foods, and this created a sense of sharing and community that made their lives more bearable. I also sensed that they realized that these skills of qi cultivation, awareness, and creative expression gave them a sense of hope that they could grow and change, even if facing long prison sentences."[9]

Recover Your Creative Birthright[10]

If children grew up according to early indications,
we should have nothing but geniuses.
Johann Wolfgang von Goethe (1749–1832),
German poet and polymath[11]

Who are the most imaginative, playful, curious, passionate beings? Children! Every healthy child is born with an unlimited potential to create. And children are pure manifestations of creative energy. That's why they are all charismatic. The adults we call geniuses are those who have maintained their childlike charisma by continuing to cultivate their imagination, curiosity, passion, and playfulness as they grow up, and then channeled it all into their chosen discipline.

Sigmund Freud wrote a book about Leonardo da Vinci in which he noted, "The great Leonardo remained like a child for the whole of his life. . . . Even as an adult he continued to play, and this was why he often appeared uncanny and incomprehensible to his contemporaries."[12] At age eighty-five, Nobel Laureate Murray Gell-Mann displays a marvelously playful attitude and a wickedly sharp wit. Gell-Mann explains, "I chose the name 'Quark' [the elementary particle he conceived that revolutionized physics] because it was quirky and amusing. I'm driven by insatiable curiosity about the nature of the universe and I've always viewed my work as a delightful game."[13]

Like da Vinci and Gell-Mann, you were born with a neural and energetic endowment that gives you unlimited creative potential. We inherit a birthright of genius, but with rare exceptions, most of us are de-geniused. How do we get de-geniused? And what can we do to get re-geniused?

Most of us begin to lose touch with our creative birthright at school. If you have a copy of your first-grade class photograph, dig it out and take a look. Most children in the first grade display a fearless, natural curiosity and openness, reflected in an upright, alert posture, bright eyes, and big smiles. First graders sit like happy lollipops! Take a few moments right now and imagine yourself with the openness, energy, and innocence of that child.

If you look at your photographs from fourth or fifth grade, you will probably see a decline in poise. Kids start hunching their shoulders and tensing their faces as they become older, so that by the time most students reach high school, their bodies are both slumped and tense. This decline is partly a function of adjusting to a growing body while sitting in one place for a long time, day after day, year after year. But the greatest cause of this loss of poise, and the de-geniusing that accompanies it, is the fear of failure or embarrassment.

Think back to your first few years at school. Can you recall a time when the teacher asked a question, and one of the children in your class waved his or her hand wildly: "Ooh ooh—I know!" Then he or she blurted out an original, creative answer, but the overworked, beleaguered teacher said, "No! Wrong! That's not the answer I was looking for!" Or maybe one of your classmates asked a really creative, off-the-wall question, and the teacher responded, "That's a silly question!" And all the kids in the class started laughing. On that day a little voice in everyone's head said, "Never, ever, ever yell out a wrong answer or ask a creative question again!"

The pressure to get the "right" answer and parrot back what the person in authority wants or expects us to say often gets worse when we go to college. Did you ever have a professor who wrote the text and expected you to paraphrase it back to him in order to get good marks?

As philosopher and poet Ralph Waldo Emerson noted, "Colleges hate geniuses, just as convents hate saints."[14]

Most of us learn that doing well in school, at all levels, is not about self-expression, originality, or creativity. Rather, it's about getting the right answer, pleasing authority, and avoiding the humiliation and ostracism associated with mistakes and failing. The result is that we often develop a negative attitude toward activities or subjects that don't come easily. When the right answer isn't obvious, it becomes all too easy to shrug and say, "I can't do this. I don't have the talent." This phenomenon creates a negative, self-fulfilling prophecy that locks in the habits and creative blocks associated with a fixed mindset.

Pioneering psychologist Abraham Maslow (1908–1970) said, "The key question isn't 'What fosters creativity?' But it is why in God's name isn't everyone creative? Where was the human potential lost? How was it crippled? I think therefore a good question might be not why do people create? But why do people not create or innovate? We have got to abandon that sense of amazement in the face of creativity, as if it were a miracle if anybody created anything."[15]

You were born with the potential for genius, and embracing the creative mindset is the beginning of re-geniusing. And since you were born with this mindset, and with an abundant supply of creative energy, all you need to do to re-enter this kingdom of heaven is to "change and become like little children" (Matthew 18:3).

In a paper entitled "Child's Play: Facilitating the Originality of Creative Output by a Priming Manipulation," Darya L. Zabelina and Michael D. Robinson reported on a study of seventy-six subjects, divided into two groups. Both groups were asked to write, for ten minutes, about what they would do with a free day. But just one of the groups was asked to imagine that they were seven years old and that school had been cancelled.

The group that viewed the free day from their adult perspective wrote about mundane prospects, like completing chores, resting, or getting extra work done. The group that envisioned themselves as children wrote wonderfully imaginative essays about the fun and learning they would enjoy.

After the writing exercise, both groups were given standard tests of creative thinking ability, such as the Alternate Use Test (asking questions such as, "Think of as many uses as you possibly can for a paper clip") that measures creative fluency (the number of ideas generated), flexibility (the number of different categories of the ideas), and originality (the extent to which the ideas were unique). The group who imagined that they were children scored significantly higher on all dimensions of the test.[16] In an interview with *Psychology Today*, Zabelina emphasized the importance of "applying a childlike mind-set to our daily lives." Zabelina concludes, "It's about giving yourself permission to explore and free time to play. It would not just increase your creativity—it would also motivate you to create."[17]

Albert Einstein's insights into the universe were possible because he "gave himself permission to explore and free time to play." He wrote, "The pursuit of truth and beauty is a sphere of activity in which we are permitted to remain children all our lives."[18] Einstein (1879–1955) maintained the curiosity and openness of a child throughout his life, and combined it with the discipline and analytical abilities of a dedicated scholar. He loved to have fun by playing the role of absentminded professor. One day as he walked across the Princeton campus, he passed a group of undergraduates. They greeted the great man, and he asked them, "From which direction have I come?" One of the students responded, "You were walking from the dining hall toward the lab." "Ah," responded Einstein. "Thank you. That means I must have already had lunch."

Playfulness is a characteristic of the most creative people in all walks of life. Matt Groening, the creator of *The Simpsons,* explains the secret of his creativity: "Most grownups forgot what it was like to be a kid. I vowed that I would never forget."[19]

"Genius," as French poet Charles Baudelaire (1821–1867) expressed it, is nothing less than, "the recovery of childhood at will."[20]

Qi Cultivation to Support Your Re-Geniusing

Qi is our cosmic fuel.

Dean Y. Deng, MD[21]

We are all born with a natural endowment of creative energy, but as the decades roll by, it tends to fade. What if you could reawaken your original birthright?

You can!

All of the qi-cultivation practices in this book are designed to support the renaissance of your original creative power. In this meditation, you will use your imagination to go back to your childhood, when your original qi was very strong and flowing freely. You will then bring this vibrant energy back across the decades to your present chronological age. This is a simple, elegant way to "recover your childhood at will."

 ## Recovering-Your-Childhood Qi Meditation

Start in the basic standing posture: feet shoulder width apart, tip of the tongue on the palatal junction, spine supple, aligned on the vertical axis, knees slightly bent, lower back releasing downward.

Extend and round your arms in front of your body, as if you were holding a large ball of energy (the same arm position as the Love Posture in the Three Treasures Standing Meditation Practice). Enjoy three slow, deep breaths into your belly. Your eyes may be open or closed.

Keeping your arms raised, imagine yourself as a happy child. Men go back to age six, and women to age seven. (These are the ages that the sages believed we are at the peak of our unadulterated qi.) Remember or construct, with as much detail as you can, an image of a happy moment, a time when your natural qi was strong and vital. See this happy, radiant, innocent, smiling version of yourself there in front of you. Inhale deeply, and as you exhale, imagine letting go of all the baggage associated with aging, as though you were taking off a heavy cloak. Then see yourself walking into and fully inhabiting the younger version of yourself. Be this beautiful child as you continue the meditation.

Maintaining the Love Posture, inhale and draw the qi from the great reservoir of energy in your lower belly up through the back of your spine, through the Jade Pillow at the back of your head, to the apex point on the top of your head. And then draw it down to the point of perception, between your eyebrows.

Exhale as you project the energy of the point of perception, like a powerful fiber-optic light beam, down to the tip of your nose, the tip of your tongue, through the larynx, chest, heart, lungs, stomach, and other vital organs, to the lower belly. Deposit the energy into your lower center.

Repeat the cycle seven times, inhaling as you move the energy up, concentrating it at the point of perception, and exhaling as you return the energy to your lower center.

If your eyes were closed, open them. Begin slowly pulsing your arms, opening and closing them at the level of your abdomen, solar plexus, or chest—whatever is most comfortable. Inhale as you open your arms; exhale as you close them. Let the energy building between your hands grow into a big ball. You may experience your hands glowing with warmth.

Move your arms in and out for every year of your life up to your current chronological age, imagining the energy growing stronger with each movement. Imagine that you are restoring your original vitality. When you reach your present age, you feel revitalized, full of enthusiasm, wellness, and verve. Enjoy the feeling of renewed energy and strength throughout your whole being.

Place your palms over your lower center. End by nourishing your qi.

Invite Surprise and Wonder

In the novel *Boy's Life,* Robert McCammon writes, "We all start out knowing magic. We are born with whirlwinds, forest fires, and comets inside of us. We are all born able to sing to birds and read the clouds and see our destiny in grains of sand." But, he adds, "We get the magic educated right out of our souls. We get it churched out, spanked out, washed out, and combed out."[22]

How to rediscover the magic? Let go of what you think you know. Embrace innocence. Surrender your preconceptions. Suspend your sophistication. As the poet Rumi advises, "Sell your cleverness and buy bewilderment."[23]

In a classic Zen parable, a master invites his student for tea. The master pours the tea. The student's cup is filled, but the master continues to pour. As the cup overflows, the student cries out, "Master, my cup is full, it's overflowing." The master replies, "So it is with your mind; if you are to receive my teaching you must first empty your cup."

You can empty your cup and bring more openness to any creative challenge by playfully checking your preconceptions at the door. Try beginning any creative endeavor by writing down as many of your fixed-mindset assumptions, preconceived beliefs, and prejudices as you can. Then crumple up the paper and throw it out the door or into the wastebasket. (Actually, many of my clients seem to get a special kick out of throwing the paper at each other.)

The Samurai maxim "Expect nothing, be ready for anything" is apt for martial artists and creators alike. Our habitual patterns of thought lead to expectations that are by definition habitual and not creative. One of the keys to a creative mindset and a real secret of igniting and sustaining the fire of genius is to *open your mind to the possibility of surprise and invite the unexpected.*

Embrace Playfulness, Humor, and Laughter

Oh wondrous creatures
By what strange miracle
Do you so often not smile?
Hafiz (1325–1390), Persian poet[24]

In many situations, people are afraid to be playful, for fear of being dismissed as "not serious." They seem to believe that a tense, miserable demeanor gives the impression that hard work is being done. Over-seriousness is a harbinger of mediocrity and bureaucratic thinking. The creative mindset embraces humor because humor inspires the recovery of childhood, the heart of creativity, and because it's just more fun.

Qigong master and physician Dean Y. Deng is a powerhouse of positive, healing, creative energy. Deng was initiated into an ancient lineage of qi cultivation when he was three years old, and he went on to earn his medical degree at China's prestigious Sun Yat-Sen University of Medical Sciences. Although he spends most of his days treating patients with severe illness, he is always cheerful, and lights up a room with his beautiful smile and booming laughter. Deng comments, "A big belly laugh is one of the best ways to awaken your qi." When I asked him about the source of his remarkable healing power, he replied, as he laughed aloud, "God provides the energy, you heal yourself, you give me the money, and I get all the credit!"[25]

Why do creative people love to laugh? And how, specifically, are humor and creativity related? One hypothesis is based on what researchers call incongruity theory, which suggests that we laugh at things that defy our expectations, like surprising juxtapositions, elements that seem out of place, and double meanings. Humor creates incongruity in a way that outwits our habitual expectations and surprises our minds.

Here are two examples of humorous incongruity:

- Did you hear about the woman who drowned in a bowl of granola? She was pulled under by a powerful currant.
- I asked my trainer if he could teach me some new yoga poses. He said, "How flexible are you?" I replied, "I can't make Wednesdays or Fridays."

The setup of these jokes leads us down a path of expectation—that the woman drowned as the result of a current, not a dried fruit, and that *flexibility* refers to the physical kind instead of the scheduling kind—and then we are surprised by the punch line. Getting the jokes requires our minds to go in unexpected directions. The incongruity makes us laugh. Ha-ha!

When we have a creative insight, something very similar takes place: we are pursuing a familiar train of thought, but then we leap to an unexpected idea and make a surprising connection. Ah ha![26]

In 2004, a research team led by Dartmouth psychologist William Kelley, PhD, asked participants to watch episodes of *Seinfeld* and *The Simpsons* while the team recorded fMRI images of the participants' brain activity. Later, when researchers compared the brain scans with the timing of the participants' laughter, they found that two seconds before participants laughed at a joke (when their brains were working to get the joke), their posterior temporal lobes—the same area of the brain that helps resolve incongruities and solve problems—lit up.[27] Those findings give neurological support to what psychologists have known for several decades: exposure to comedy bolsters creativity and enhances problem-solving and workplace effectiveness.

In another classic study, psychologist Avner Ziv, PhD, arranged for high school students to listen to a recording of a comedian before taking a standardized creativity test (the same test used by Zabelina and Robinson). The students who listened to the comedian scored significantly higher than the control group on all dimensions of the test.[28]

Fred Milder, PhD, is the CEO of SolarLogic, a company dedicated to "growing the solar thermal industry for the economic and environmental benefit of all." Fred recruits people with a combination of technical brilliance and a sense of humor because, as he explains, "I look for creative contributors. People with a sense of humor, especially people who can laugh at themselves, are more creative and do a better job."[29]

Whatever your taste in humor, enjoy a regular diet of laughter: seek out cartoons, movies, and jokes that make you laugh.

Laughter is the quickest and least expensive way to take a vacation. A brief interlude of chuckling, just ten to twenty seconds, is a perfect antidote to over-seriousness. British author, critic, and theologian G. K. Chesterton (1874–1936) reminds us, "Angels can fly because they take themselves lightly."[30] Spontaneous laughter strengthens your immune system, improves your mood, and enlivens your qi.

One of the best ways to explore the relationship between humor and creativity is to improvise. Michelle James, founder of Quantum Leap Business Improv, explains, "You were born as a natural improviser. Remember the pretend worlds and games you created as a child?" James adds, "The same principles that allow improvised magic to happen on stage can be applied to your everyday life, to enhance your spontaneity, playfulness, and creativity."[31]

Another fun way to bring more laughter to your life is to record your favorite jokes and funny stories, and then share them with your friends. Here are a few to get you going:

- Two cannibals were eating a clown. One asks the other, "Does this taste funny to you?"
- A priest, a rabbi and a minister walk into a bar. The bartender asks, "Is this some kind of joke?"
- There was a man who entered a local newspaper's pun contest. He sent in ten different puns, in the hope that at least one of the puns would win. Unfortunately, no pun in ten did.
- If a parsley farmer is audited by the IRS, can they garnish his wages?

Humor isn't just a means of relieving stress; it's a key to a healthy perspective on life, enlivened qi, and a more creative mindset.

Qi Cultivation for Embracing Surprise and Humor

The source of a true smile is an awakened mind.

Thich Nhat Hanh[32]

The field of smilology is broadening its scope. Research suggests that restaurant servers who smile get bigger tips,[33] single women who smile meet more men than those who don't,[34] and people who smile more frequently may live significantly longer lives.[35] In a study entitled "Smile to See the Forest: Facially Expressed Positive Emotions Broaden Cognition," Kareem J. Johnson et al. discovered that smiling facilitates our ability to see the big picture, a very important element of creative thinking.[36]

Even without reading the scientific research, you probably would agree that smiling has many benefits. As the ancient Chinese proverb says, "Every smile makes you a day younger." Yet when I attended my first meditation class forty-two years ago, I was surprised to see that most people looked rather grim. I've observed the same phenomenon in aikido, tai chi, and yoga classes over the years.

In her book *Eat, Pray, Love,* Elizabeth Gilbert shares advice from her Balinese healer who wondered why Westerners seem so somber in pursuit of enlightenment. He asks, "Why they always look so serious in Yoga? You make serious face like this, you scare away good energy." And he advises Gilbert, "Smile with face, smile with mind, and good energy will come to you and clean away dirty energy. Even smile in your liver. . . . You can call the good energy with a smile."[37]

The following exercise is adapted from the work of qi master Michael Winn. Winn, whose natural expression is not unlike that of the Mona Lisa, offers this delightful approach to "calling the good energy with a smile." He explains:

> What is the key difference between the inner smile and
> the ordinary outer smile? The ordinary outer smile has
> an "object," someone or something you are smiling at. The
> inner smile is ultimately objectless. You might temporarily

start by smiling to some aspect of your biology, but you quickly go past that to the energy or the spirit behind the physical object. Once you contact your center of spiritual gravity, the inner smile radiates back out through the layers of your energy body and your biology and eventually out into the world. So you end up smiling like a glowing lamp, shining out from the open space within yourself, at the insides (i.e., the "subject") of all objects in the world. So you end up smiling from your inside to the insides of everything else.[38]

 ## Inner Smile Practice

The practice has two parts. You can do each on its own or one after the other, in either order.

Part 1: Smile to the Inner World

Sit or lie down. Rest your tongue gently on the palatal junction. Mindfully follow the flow of your breathing for a few breaths.

Imagine that you are smiling with every cell of your being. Allow that smile to be expressed through your face. Allow yourself to be, as poet Percy Bysshe Shelley might suggest, "arrayed in the soft light of your own smile, spreading like radiance from the cloud-surrounded moon."[39]

Now project the soft light of that smile into your bones and bone marrow. Savor the feeling of smiling into each of the parts of your being for a minimum of one full cycle of breath.

Smile into your belly and intestines.

Smile into your liver and then your kidneys.

Smile into your heart, and let the smile flow through all your blood vessels.

Smile into your genitals.

Smile into your brain and through your entire nervous system.

Smile into all your muscles and connective tissue.

Now smile again through your whole being.

Part 2: Smile to the Outer World

Begin the same way as in part 1.

Project the soft light of your smile out to your aura. Then let the energy of your smile fill the room.

Send your smile to a loved one.

Smile to your most challenging relationship.

Smile to your local community.

Smile to your country.

Smile to the whole Earth.

Let your smile fill the solar system.

Send your smile to the edge of the galaxy.

Smile to the entire universe.

Now feel the entire universe smiling back at you. Gather the wave of smiling qi in a pearl-shaped point three inches below your navel. Place your hands over that point and rest.

Feel gratitude. End by nourishing your qi. And smile.

Clarify Your Purpose

> The bigger the purpose you connect with, the greater the energy.
>
> Mingtong Gu, qi master and healer[40]

Once you realize that you are born to be creative and that you can continue to cultivate your creative energy throughout life, the big question becomes: "What do I want to create?"

In order to know what you want to create, it helps to know your purpose. Perhaps you already have a well-defined and inspiring sense of purpose. Most people find, however, that they can benefit by clarifying and energizing their sense of purpose. A clear sense of purpose makes it much easier to deal with adversity and overcome obstacles. Leonardo da Vinci counseled, "Fix your course to a star."[41] Philosopher Friedrich Nietzsche (1844–1900) advised, "He who has a why in life can bear with almost any how."[42]

What's your star, your why? What's the meaning of your life? It is, of course, to make your life meaningful. How? By knowing your purpose and striving to live in alignment with it.

Beyond the quest for shelter, food, sex, social acceptance, power, and money, why are you here?

Try this exercise: Get a pen and a blank sheet of paper and, in the next few minutes, write down your life's purpose. Even if you feel that you have no idea of your purpose, please just make something up. If you already have a well-defined purpose statement, write it out.

After completing your first draft, highlight the words in your statement that have the most resonance for you at this time.

Invest a minimum of ten minutes each day contemplating your key words and reviewing and revising your statement until you feel fully aligned with, and excited by, what you've written.

To inspire you, here are a few examples of what other people have written in response to this exercise.

Margot Borden, a psychotherapist and author of *Spirituality and Business: Exploring Possibilities for a New Management Paradigm,* wrote, "Use my intelligence, wisdom, and humor to help people unravel the web of blockages and limitations that prevent them from fulfilling their potential."

Two-time James Beard Award–winning author Karen Page wrote, "To raise awareness of the power of eating, drinking, and dining mindfully to create a healthier and more beautiful world."

Mezzo-soprano Deborah Domanski wrote, "Remind people of their connection to the divine by bringing to life the most beautiful vocal music ever written."

Jason A. Voss, content director for the Chartered Financial Analyst Institute and author of *The Intuitive Investor,* wrote, "To empower people to make more conscious choices in their lives using reason and intuition harmoniously so they can grow financially and spiritually."

Thirty-five years ago, I wrote, "Be a champion for creativity, consciousness, and compassion while savoring the joy of living."

How do you know when you've found your purpose? It's easier to get up in the morning! You experience brighter, stronger qi throughout your entire being. Some people start crying when they express their purpose for the first time, and others break into deep laughter. Either way, finding your purpose enlivens your energy, and enlivening your energy will help you fulfill your purpose.

David Lamb is a fourth-generation business owner and a wonderfully creative leader. His purpose statement is simple and clear: "Have fun, make money, do right." He says, "All our endeavors must meet all three criteria. The last one is the most important."

David refers to his purpose statement playfully as "the Mantra." In one of our many conversations, he explained, "Our Mantra evolved from my taking six companies through bankruptcy in five countries in 2001. We went broke long before it became fashionable. We bounced back from adversity, guided by the Mantra. Our people buy into this way of thinking. They love it. And it brings us together."

David adds, "Of course, it is easy to say and, sometimes, hard to apply. But we are committed to bridging the gap."

As you clarify and refine the expression of your purpose, you will probably notice increased incidents of what Jung referred to as synchronicity, "an acausal connecting principal." In other words, you will experience more meaningful coincidences.[43] The notion of synchronicity is expressed in the proverb "When the student is ready, the teacher will appear."[44] If, for example, you decide you want to be a landscape painter, don't be too surprised when your seatmate on your next flight is an instructor of landscape painting.

Every time I've decided wholeheartedly that learning something was part of my purpose, a superb teacher of that discipline has appeared. The key is wholeheartedness. *Wholeheartedness organizes your perception to follow your purpose.* You notice connections you might have missed previously. This is why clarity of purpose is an essential element of the creative mindset.

Wholeheartedness is also the secret of discovering and clarifying your purpose. While you are doing the exercise, your purpose is to discover and clarify your purpose. And refining and aligning with purpose is a process that continues throughout life. Sometimes, people start out in life with a clear sense of purpose, but as they face the challenges of making a living and the disappointments and heartbreaks that are inevitable parts of life, they lose touch with it. Remembering, clarifying, and enlivening your purpose are essential elements of re-geniusing.

Qi Cultivation for Realizing and Aligning with Your Core Purpose

The term *university* arose from the ideal of the pursuit of universal knowledge. Although we usually associate the notion of the universal or Renaissance person (*Uomo Universale* in Italian) with fifteenth-century Florence in general and with Leonardo da Vinci in particular, the ideal of well-rounded excellence is cherished in traditional Chinese culture and was articulated and advocated by Confucius (551–479 BCE) and Mencius (372–289 BCE) among others.

Mingtong Gu is a contemporary example of a universal/Renaissance man. A photographer, videographer, and performance artist, he is also a gifted healer and engaging presenter. He holds an MA in mathematics from the University of California (San Diego) and an MFA from Ohio State University. As a child, he suffered from scoliosis and asthma, and healed himself through qigong practice. In the process he discovered his own life purpose: "Realizing true happiness and creativity by aligning mind, body, heart, and spirit."[45] I asked him to share his wisdom, to help you discover, clarify, and align with your life purpose now.

He responded, "The secret of discovering your deeper purpose is to connect with the source energy, with qi. Knowledge of your purpose doesn't come through analysis, but rather it is an intuitive, direct, and complete knowing."[46]

Mingtong advises that you do whatever practice appeals to you the most, to connect with universal qi. You might, for example, do the Three Treasures Standing Meditation Practice on page 33 or the Inner Smile Practice on page 93. He suggests that after your qi cultivation practice, you ask yourself, "What is my true source of fulfillment?" He explains, "When you connect to source energy and focus that energy on the question of clarifying your purpose, it becomes clearer. You will align your purpose with the source of all creativity."[47]

Mingtong adds, "Become an artist with source energy. Paint the picture of what you want your life to be. Open beyond all limitation. Be the creator of your life."[48]

Create Your Own Logo and Motto

You can deepen the effectiveness of the purpose-definition exercise by creating your own logo and motto. A logo and motto serve as powerful mnemonics that keep you aligned with your purpose.

In Renaissance Italy, princes, nobles, and scholars all created a symbolic representation of their purpose known as an *impresa*. Coats of arms began as battle standards in the rest of Europe, but eventually evolved into symbols of a noble family's identity or purpose.

In contemporary times the corporate logo represents an organization's identity as it reinforces their brand. Think about the logos with which you are familiar. Perhaps the most recognized and ubiquitous logo in the world today is the Nike swoosh. The shape evokes movement, and its name evokes the sound of movement. Nike's purpose is to "clothe the athletes of the world," and the company believes "if you have a body, you're an athlete." Its logo serves as an internal unifying force for its employees and an instant brand identifier for its customers.

Logos can be very powerful, and you needn't be a noble or a corporation to have one. You can clarify your purpose in a more memorable and creative way by developing your own impresa or logo. Begin by getting some scrap paper and a pen and doodling symbols and images that you feel are representative of your identity and purpose. Play with this exercise for a few minutes every day until you create something that resonates for you.

Webster's Dictionary defines a motto as "a short expression of a guiding principle." Take your purpose statement and translate it into a motto. What's the difference between the two? The motto is usually even more inspiring and memorable. Nike, for example, crafted an unforgettable motto to go with its logo: "Just do it."

Images and key words are the key ingredients of memory. By crafting a core image (logo) and essential key words (motto) that express your purpose, you are much more likely to remember and therefore live your purpose.

To fuel your imagination, here are some examples of great mottos:

> My motto was always to keep swinging. Whether I
> was in a slump or feeling badly or having trouble off
> the field, the only thing to do was keep swinging.
> *Hank Aaron, American baseball player*
> *and National Baseball Hall of Fame inductee[49]*

> I wish to work miracles.
> *Leonardo da Vinci[50]*

> Expedite serendipity.
> *Shirley Ann Jackson, PhD,*
> *President of Rensselaer Polytechnic Institute[51]*

> *Illegitimi non carborundum.*
> *Latin for "Don't let the bastards get you down."*

> Imagine.
> *John Lennon (1940–1980)*

Think.
IBM

Think different.
Apple

Strengthen Your Confusion Endurance

Whatever inspiration is, it's born from a continuous "I don't know."
Wislawa Szymborska (1923–2012), Polish Nobel laureate in literature[52]

The ability to embrace ambiguity and endure confusion is one of the most distinguishing characteristics of the creative mindset. Leonardo da Vinci understood this five hundred years ago. His *Mona Lisa* is the most famous work of art in human history, renowned for her mysterious smile. Why is she smiling? The best way to discover this for yourself is to assume Mona's posture and imitate her famous smile. Try this for thirty seconds now.

How do you feel when you smile like Mona Lisa? I asked this question to a group of eighty gifted children in Rappahannock County, Virginia, a few years ago. The children embraced the exercise and entered deeply into the imitation. After a few moments, a girl sitting in the back of the room raised her hand and said, "She's got a secret." And then a boy in the front exclaimed, "She knows that everything has an opposite!" And then the children offered examples—light and dark, good and bad, night and day, boys and girls, life and death.

When I led the same exercise with a corporate group recently, one person responded, "I read in the *Wall Street Journal* that the famous smile was caused by a dental problem."

The gifted boys and girls did a much better job of perceiving Mona Lisa's expression of perspective in the face of mystery. Mona's fame, in addition to the unprecedented mastery in her execution, rests on the ambiguity that da Vinci creates, the sense of dynamic tension.

The ability to accept the unknown is even more important now than it was during the Renaissance. In the 1980s corporations began to seek managers with a high "tolerance for ambiguity." More recently, *Forbes* described tolerance for ambiguity as "The One Key Trait for Successful Entrepreneurs."[53] In the classic work *The Authoritarian Personality*, sociologist Theodor Adorno (1903–1969) and colleagues introduced the idea of ambiguity intolerance—a tendency to experience "psychological discomfort or threat" in response to circumstances that an individual interprets as vague, uncertain, or incomplete.[54] Ambiguity intolerance is a symptom of the fixed mindset.

Psychologists define three dimensions of ambiguity: novelty, complexity, and perceived insolubility. In other words, if its new, complicated, and you don't have any idea how to solve it, you experience ambiguity. The creative process, in art or business or any aspect of life, involves finding something new, simplifying the complex, and discovering solutions that are unexpected.

I suggest replacing the notion of tolerating ambiguity with the idea of embracing it. Our world is changing so fast, and life is becoming ever more complex. As change and complexity multiply, what happens to the level of ambiguity in our lives? Of course, it increases.

How can you develop your ability to embrace ambiguity if you experience it as a source of psychological discomfort or threat? The same way you shift from a fixed mindset to a growth mindset: by practicing self-observation and changing your internal dialogue. Here's a review of the four steps for shifting to a growth mindset applied to overcoming ambiguity intolerance:

Step 1: Observe the voice of your ambiguity intolerance.

Step 2: Choose how to interpret a situation.

Step 3: Answer the voice of your ambiguity intolerance
      with the voice of your creative mindset.

Step 4: Take the action that is based on the creative mindset.

Strengthening your confusion endurance is also a matter of changing your expectations. If you want to be more creative, and you understand that, by definition, something creative is unknown, then you begin to expect and embrace the unknown rather than avoiding it.

Creators on Qi

Vanda North

Former president of the International Society for Accelerated Learning and Teaching, author, and international business consultant Vanda North is a powerhouse of creative energy. She enthuses, "I've been a student of various forms of qi cultivation throughout my life. There are several internal factors that are important to awaken the flow of qi to cultivate creativity, but mindset is most critical. Self-concept, self-talk, motivation, and confidence all interact, either synergistically or antagonistically, to profoundly influence the quality of our lives and our ability to create."[55]

North utilizes a simple eight-minute process (one minute for each of the eight steps) that she developed with her colleague Richard Israel for strengthening the creative mindset.

The first two steps get your body and mind attuned and ready for optimization: Breathe into your belly, allowing it to expand as you inhale and settle back as you exhale. Then attend to the present moment. Look at a second hand on a timepiece and think of the word *one* for a full minute. When an intruding thought arises, move up a number. Notice what number you reach by the end of the minute. The object is to keep your "score" at one.

The next two steps involve a review of your mindset and performance: First, look back over the past twenty-four hours to see where you might have acted or spoken in a more positive, helpful, or creative manner. Count these times on your nondominant hand. Next, look back over the past twenty-four hours to see where you did perform in a positive, helpful, or creative way. Count these times on your dominant hand.

The next two steps focus on preparing for optimization: First, check in with your breathing, bodily sensations, and feelings in this moment. Next, draw in creative energy as you inhale deeply into your belly, and as you exhale, release any remnants of stress. Focus on the attitudes and qualities you wish to embody.

The final two steps focus on envisioning the future you desire: First, project ahead over the next twenty-four hours. How would you like to think, feel, and act? Create a positive vision of your upcoming day. Then bask in a sense of gratitude for all that you have received and may receive. Gratitude strengthens your immune system, improves your mood, and inspires the healthy flow of qi.

North comments, "This process arose as a response to very stressful circumstances in my life. My relationship with the person who I thought was my life partner disintegrated, my business of twenty years went into liquidation, and my closest and dearest relative died. Facing my sixtieth birthday, I had to dig deep for creative solutions to many problems. Although I struggled for many months with confusion, hurt, and anxiety, I knew that cultivating qi was the key to survive and thrive."[56]

How did North respond? She celebrated her sixtieth birthday by climbing Mt. Kilimanjaro to raise funds for her local hospital's charity drive. She placed in the top ten in the over-fifty women's lightweight world ergometer (stationary rowing machine) championships. She ran a 10K race for charity, found the love of her life and got married, and then published a book about the effects of attitude on qi.

As she approaches her seventieth birthday, North exults, "I'm stronger, and my life is better than it has ever been before." She concludes, "A creative mindset is most important when we face uncertainty and adversity. The creative mindset inspires and sustains the flow of qi, and qi then fuels the creative process that empowers us to thrive."[57]

Move Beyond Either-Or Thinking

Please take a few minutes and note your immediate response to each of the following questions:

- Is it better to be a planner or an improviser?
- Which is more critical to organizational success: leadership or management?
- Is it more important to do good or to make money?
- Which is more important for personal fulfillment: feminine qualities or masculine qualities?
- Is disruptive innovation good or bad?
- Which is more valuable to humanity: science or art?
- Is it better to be serious or playful?
- Which is more important in the creative process: imagination or knowledge?

Each of the questions above presents what logicians refer to as a false dichotomy, also known as the either-or fallacy. This is a way of posing a problem or question in which the alternatives considered are limited unnecessarily. Many people limit their creative power by framing questions in this way.

Either-or thinking is useful when we have simple, clear choices, such as, "At the T-junction do I turn left or right?" or "If there are two candidates on the ballot, which one gets my vote?" But either-or thinking isn't so helpful in dealing with more complex problems. IBM's recently published Creative Leadership Study came to a similar conclusion. It found that "to succeed in an increasingly interconnected world, creative leaders avoid choosing between unacceptable alternatives. Instead, they use the power inherent in these dualities to invent new assumptions and create new models geared to an ever-changing world."[58]

So move beyond limiting, either-or ways of looking at yourself and the world. The creative mindset reframes either-or propositions in order to stimulate more productive thinking. For example, either-or questions such as "Is it better to be a planner or an improviser?" and "Which is more critical to organizational success: leadership or management?" can be rephrased as follows:

- How can I discover the ideal relationship between planning and improvisation?
- What practical skills need to be cultivated in our organization to ensure the most productive balance between management and leadership?

The creative mindset uses the power inherent in dualities to invent new assumptions and create new models. So be a planner *and* an improviser, a manager *and* a leader. Discover the balance between seriousness and play. Seek ways to make money by doing good. Integrate intuition and analysis, imagination and knowledge, yin and yang. And remember to smile like Mona.

Qi Cultivation to Strengthen Confusion Endurance and Move Beyond Either-Or Thinking

Movement 4, *Sfumato,* from the Da Vinci Qi Practice on page 56 is very helpful in strengthening your confusion endurance and your ability to move beyond either-or thinking. You can also support these essential elements of the creative mindset by experimenting with this meditation.

Paradoxical Energy Meditation[59]

In this meditation you'll contemplate three energetic paradoxes. As you entertain these oppositional energetic flows and then reconcile them, you support your ability to remain poised in the face of uncertainty.

Begin in the basic standing posture. Smile like the Mona Lisa.

Paradox 1. Sink your energy down through your Bubbling Spring points in the feet into the depths of the earth. Be sure to maintain a lengthening spine as you send your energy down, down, down. After projecting your energy down for a minute, shift your awareness to get a sense of the ground pushing up to support you. Imagine a sense of upthrust from the earth, supporting you in a buoyant and effortless manner. After focusing on the uplifting energy of the earth for a minute, allow your awareness to rest, for the next minute, in a neutral place between sinking down and being buoyed up.

Paradox 2. As you stand, imagine yourself as an immovable mountain. Solid, dense, rock steady, one with the earth, you stand majestically, like the greatest mountain you've ever seen. Hold this for one minute. For the next minute, imagine that you are utterly mobile in every cell, featherlike in your pliability and virtual weight-lessness. Now embrace both qualities simultaneously and enjoy the paradox for one minute.

Paradox 3. Direct your attention out to the cosmos. Envision the edge of the earth's atmosphere and then the boundary of our solar system. Go beyond, to the outer borders of our galaxy, and then send your imagination to the farthest reaches of the universe. Enjoy this imaginative space travel for a minute. Then, as you inhale, imagine concentrating all the qi of the universe into a pearl-sized sphere at the center of your lower center. As you exhale, allow the qi to distill and concentrate into an infinitely powerful source of vitality. After one minute of focusing on the pearl within, embrace the center of your being and the whole universe simultaneously.

Finish by refreshing your Mona Lisa smile and nourishing your qi.

Assume Chutzpah

> Unfold your own myth.
>
> Rumi[60]

In act 3, scene 4, of Shakespeare's *Hamlet,* the Prince of Denmark beseeches his mother to "[a]ssume a virtue, if you have it not." This is Shakespeare's way of saying "fake it until you make it." The *Urban Dictionary* explains that this phrase means "to act like you are something so you can, in fact, become that thing." Hamlet emphasizes this point by adding, "For use almost can change the stamp of nature." And, he concludes, "[h]abit can change even one's natural instincts, and either rein in the devil in us, or kick him out."

Shakespeare's advice echoes the idea originated by the Greek philosopher Aristotle (384–322 BCE) that we acquire a particular quality by acting in a particular way.[61] In other words, we become ethical by acting ethically, and brave by acting bravely.

And we become creative by acting creatively.

This is the chutzpah principle of creativity.[62] *Chutzpah* is a Yiddish word that can be interpreted to mean audacity or nerve in the face of uncertainty. The closest word in the American vernacular is *moxie*.

Chutzpah is a critical element in the success of people from many walks of life. Jack Dorsey, the founder of Twitter and Square, won the *Wall Street Journal's* "Innovator of the Year" Award in 2012. In a 2013 interview with the television show *60 Minutes,* he explained the role of chutzpah in his early career. As a teenager, Dorsey loved monitoring police and fire dispatches (the brevity and clarity of the dispatcher's words eventually inspired him to limit Tweets to 140 characters). Dorsey wanted to work for a major dispatch company in New York City, but they didn't post information publicly on how to apply for a job. So he hacked into their computer system and then wrote them a note to ask for a job.

As he told *60 Minutes* interviewer Lara Logan, "I found a way into the website . . . I found a security hole . . . And I emailed them and I said, 'You have a security hole. Here's how to fix it. And I write dispatch software.' And . . ."

Lara Logan: "And they hired you?"

Jack Dorsey: "And they hired me a week later. And it was a dream come true."

A self-made billionaire, Dorsey's long-term goal is to be mayor of New York City. I wouldn't bet against him.

Irish writer and wit Oscar Wilde (1854–1900) had abundant chutz-pah. On a visit to the United States, a customs officer asked him if he had anything to declare. Wilde responded, "I have nothing to declare except my genius."[63]

Academy Award–winning actor Jeremy Irons explained the secret of his early success: "I succeeded on a sort of chutzpah and charm. No technique at all, didn't know what I was doing, but it worked."[64]

A recent article in *Forbes* described chutzpah as "the new charisma." *Forbes* interviewed Rabbi Tzvi Freeman, who describes it as "a kind of cosmic attitude, as though there's nothing really there stopping you from doing whatever you want."[65]

Amy Elizabeth Fox is the co-founder of Mobius Executive Leader-ship, a successful boutique training and consulting firm. She explained how chutzpah helped launch her business:

> Long before we had even one client engagement, I spoke
> about Mobius as if it were already in place, with hundreds
> of practitioners, because that is how I envisioned it. Our
> very first trainer-certification seminar had over thirty
> people even though we didn't yet have a book of business.
> Once we had declared without reservation that we were
> going forward, the job of backfilling reality became much
> easier. I guess it took major chutzpah for us to act as
> though we had an established, successful firm when all we
> really had was a dream, but that's probably a significant
> factor in the dream becoming real.[66]

Amy's story is a living example of the application of the advice from leg-endary entrepreneur Sir Richard Branson: "If somebody offers you an amazing oportunity but you are not sure you can do it, say yes—then learn to do it later."[67]

You don't have to feel confident and creative; just act as though you are. Ask yourself, "If I were really creative and confident, how would I approach this situation?" People with chutzpah make a habit of think-ing creatively when presented with a question or challenge for which an answer is not immediately available. When your first reaction to a problem is, "Gee, I don't know," you can awaken your creative power by asking, "Well, if I did know, what would I say?"

There is, of course, a critical difference between an informed guess, cre-ative association, intelligent speculation, and total baloney. Nevertheless, you can liberate your unlimited capacity for creativity with a little chutzpah.

Be Courageous and Persevere

> Courage is the capacity to meet the anxiety which arises
> as one achieves freedom.
> Rollo May (1909–1994), American psychologist[68]

"What if" questions are wonderful tools for creative thinking, but they can also be used to sabotage our endeavors:

- What if I commit myself to learning to paint or sing or dance or write, and it turns out that I'm terrible?
- What if I follow my dream and start my company, and it goes bankrupt? Won't that prove I'm a failure?
- What if I propose my new idea to my boss, and he rejects it?
- What if I try this new recipe I created, and no one likes it?
- What if I allow myself to fall in love, and I get my heart broken again?

Creativity in any area of life requires courage. If it's creative, it's a risk. There's always the possibility of rejection.

We tend to think of heroism as a feat of derring-do—rescuing hos-tages or pulling someone from a burning building—but the courage to make inner changes, to face anxiety directly, is equally heroic. The process of shifting out of a fixed mindset to embrace a creative one will, for most people, generate significant anxiety. Rescuing the creative self that has been held hostage by the fixed mindset, pulling your dreams out of the quicksand of fear, and committing to a more creative life are acts of courage.

The word *courage* comes from the Latin root *cor,* meaning "heart." Creativity requires heart, the willingness to trust yourself even as you recognize that you could be wrong. It also requires the strength to trust yourself in the face of resistance, which you will surely encounter if your invention, idea, painting, or project is truly creative.

In the research for our book *Innovate Like Edison,* Sarah Miller Caldicott and I interviewed many members of the National Inventors Hall of Fame, including Donald Keck, the co-inventor of optical fiber; Robert Langer, inventor of pharmaceutical transdermal delivery systems; and Helen Free, co-inventor of dip-and-read diagnostic tests. All of these successful creators explained that, early in their careers, before they were famous, they encountered tremendous resistance to their creative initiatives. Edison himself faced intense criticism from many directions, including the head of the British Royal Institution of Science, who proclaimed that his idea of practical incandescence was "utterly impossible!" One year later, on November 4, 1879, Edison applied for his basic patent on the incandescent light. And soon the whole world was illuminated.[69]

If your invention, idea, painting, or project is truly creative, then there's a good chance that you will experience resistance and criticism. People may even laugh at you. But just because people laugh at you doesn't mean that you are a misunderstood genius. As Carl Sagan wryly explains, "But the fact that some geniuses were laughed at does not imply that all who are laughed at are geniuses. They laughed at Columbus, they laughed at Fulton, they laughed at the Wright brothers. But they also laughed at Bozo the Clown."[70]

Creativity requires courage precisely because, whether you're a genius or not, some people will still laugh at and oppose you. Moreover, even if what you create is magnificent, there's no guarantee that you will be recognized and rewarded proportionally. There are brilliant people in every field, from painting and music to software and physics, who aren't well known, and there are others in those fields whose renown exceeds their contributions. Creativity requires the courage to live from your guiding principles, to guide your life primarily from your intrinsic truth, rather than being a slave to convention, external pressure, or potential or real rewards.

Yes, your creative mindset will help to maximize your opportunities; yes, as Louis Pasteur (1822–1895) observed, chance does favor the prepared mind, and those with a creative mindset are better prepared.[71] And, chance, luck, or karma—whatever you choose to call it—does play a role in the outcomes we experience. *But whatever your level of results, reward, and recognition, your life will be a success if you are true to your own creative path.*

Qi Cultivation for Chutzpah, Courage, and Perseverance

Courage and perseverance are essential qualities for warriors. Many qi-cultivation practices began as a way to help martial artists prepare for and survive combat. Over the years they have been adapted to help all of us prepare to be courageous and to persevere in the face of the difficulties of daily life, and especially when we need the chutzpah to overcome creative challenges. This classic practice supports a feeling of assertiveness, courage, and dignity without aggression.

 ## The Creative Warrior Draws the Bow

Begin with your hands in prayer position in front of your middle center. Take a wide stance, feet about twice shoulder width apart (find the distance that is comfortable for you).

With a lengthening spine, sink your body by bending your knees, and extend your left arm out to the left side. Your right hand forms a soft fist and pulls back to the right shoulder nest as though you were drawing a bowstring. The tip of the left index finger moves toward your left thumb, without touching it, to form a C shape. Gaze through the gap between your index and middle fingers.

Allow your heart to open, and enjoy the dynamic tension between your extended left hand and the elbow of your right arm, which is stretching in the opposite direction.

To shift to the other side, begin with a blink of your eyes. Then sweep your left hand back to the center of your body. Allow your right hand to intersect with the left to form a V shape, with your right hand on the inside. Then extend your right hand out to the right side and pull your left fist back to the left shoulder nest. Look through the space between your right index and middle fingers, and remember to keep your heart open. (See figure 2.3.)

Repeat the pose seven times on each side. Finish by nourishing your qi.

figure 2.3   The Creative Warrior Draws the Bow

Appreciate Beauty, Sensory Delights, and Natural Wonders

> Beauty itself is but the sensible image of the Infinite.
>
> George Bancroft (1800–1891), American statesman and historian[72]

In his *Symposium,* Plato (427–347 BCE) gives advice on how best to nurture the soul. He advises us to appreciate beauty in the external world, whether in art, science, or nature, in order to deepen our connection with the beauty within.[73] If you nurture your mind and heart with beauty in different forms, you will feed your soul and empower your creativity.

In our mass-market, lowest-common-denominator, spam-infested world, beauty isn't the default setting. The creative mindset seeks out and celebrates beauty on a daily basis. Like Plato, Leonardo da Vinci understood that the impressions we experience every day serve as nourishment for the soul, and that without conscious attention, it's all too easy for us to take in the sensory equivalent of junk food.

Fortunately, we now have unprecedented access to the sensory treasures of the world. We can easily, and with minimal expense, enjoy beautiful music, food, wine, and art—and, in the process, enrich the quality of our lives and strengthen our creative mindset. And we can make the positive effects of these beautiful things more memorable by practicing comparative appreciation.[74]

When you listen to multiple versions of a musical composition or compare wines in a flight, your mind attunes to the differences and similarities among them. You begin to notice subtleties, and you deepen your recall for the pleasurable experience. The key to getting the most out of comparative appreciation is to suspend your concern about making an accurate critical analysis and focus instead on contemplating open-ended questions such as: How do I experience this (music, wine, art, food, aroma)? What sensations, feelings, and impressions does this experience inspire or evoke?

The beauty of all these questions is that they have no wrong answers. As we free ourselves from the fear of saying something wrong or embarrassing, we experience deeper appreciation and enjoyment. We refine our senses and nurture our creative awareness.

Appreciation is an art in itself. You don't have to write or perform music to experience its creative essence. You needn't pick up a brush to be transformed by the power of a masterpiece painting. And you don't have to be a winemaker, chef, or chocolatier to be enlivened by the sensory delights of great wines, fine cuisine, or gourmet chocolates. Mindfully listening to music, appreciating art, or consciously savoring delectable smells and tastes can awaken your connection with the source of creativity.

Philosopher of science and poet Jacob Bronowski (1908–1974) explains that the creative essence of a work of art or a scientific discovery "exists in two moments of vision: the moment of appreciation as much as that of creation; for the appreciator must see the movement, wake to the echo which was started in the creation of the work. In the moment of appreciation . . . [W]e re-enact the creative act, and we ourselves make the discovery again."[75]

In other words, in appreciating beauty, we meet its creator in the moment of creation. That's why it's also a great idea to nurture your creative mindset by appreciating the beauty of nature.

Geniuses throughout history have celebrated the power of nature's inspiration. Leonardo advised his students to contemplate the beauty of nature when faced with a creative challenge. Murray Gell-Mann explains, "What is especially striking and remarkable is that in fundamental physics a beautiful or elegant theory is more likely to be right than a theory that is inelegant." And Murray adds, "Throughout my life, I've nurtured my appreciation of beauty and elegance by spending significant time in nature."[76]

Contemporary science is beginning to validate the intuitive understanding of these great minds. In a study conducted jointly by researchers from the universities of Utah and Kansas, a group of fifty-six people who spent four to six days on an Outward Bound nature experience, disconnected from all electronics, showed a 50 percent increase in performance on creativity tests. A follow-up study found that spending just three hours in nature led to a 20 percent improvement.[77] As naturalist John Muir reminds us, "Climb the mountains and get their good tidings; nature's peace will flow into you as sunshine flows into trees. The winds will blow their own freshness into you, and the storms their energy, while cares will drop off like autumn leaves."[78]

Qi Cultivation for Appreciating Beauty, Sensory Delights, and Natural Wonders

Movement 3 from the Da Vinci Qi Practice, *Sensazione,* is a perfect way to cleanse your doors of perception so that you can experience the sense of infinite wonder and beauty that inspires creativity.

Invoke the Muse

> Some things you will think of yourself . . .
> some things God will put into your mind.
>
> Homer[79]

How can you prepare yourself to function at the highest level of creativity? *Combine chutzpah with humility.* In any creative endeavor begin by asking, wholeheartedly, for inspiration and insight. When you get stuck or frustrated, ask for help. As you near completion, ask for guidance. Who are you asking? If you believe in God, ask God. If you believe in a Great Spirit, a Divine Mother, or a Universal Mind, then ask the Spirit, Mother, or Mind. If you don't believe in any of that, then just ask for a creative source to guide you. Vincent van Gogh (1853–1890) expressed this very well when he wrote, "I can very well do without God both in my life and in my painting, but I cannot, suffering as I am, do without something which is greater than I am, which is my life, the power to create."[80]

Direct your appeal to a creative power, something greater than your ego, however you conceive it. Whether you think of the higher power as divinely inspired or as an expression of your own intuitive gift, you'll discover that *sincerely* asking for guidance liberates you from the constricting effects of the fixed mindset. Asking for guidance, and listening deeply, gives you access to vast creative power. As Jung explained, "Creative power is mightier than its possessor."[81]

Do not underestimate the might of a wholehearted appeal to the source of creativity. And when you make such an appeal, be accountable for doing something with what you receive. As G. K. Chesterton admonishes, "Never invoke the gods unless you really want them to appear. It annoys them very much."[82]

Be careful that your appeal isn't a demand. Inspiration can't be forced. You meet the demand for creative insight by surrendering your idea of what you think you need and opening to something you don't know.

Ask. Let go. Listen. Be patient. And keep working on your craft as you wait.

There's another paradox here. You, as an individual, remain fully accountable for what you create. You must learn the craft associated with your discipline. As composer Johannes Brahms (1833–1897) expressed it, "Without craftsmanship, inspiration is a mere reed shaken in the wind."[83] You must provide the effort, commitment, and diligence. And while taking full responsibility, surrender your attachment, empty yourself, and ask for inspiration and guidance.

The idea that the secret of creativity involves surrendering to a higher power has ancient origins. According to Greek mythology, Zeus, the god of unlimited energy, made love with Mnemosyne, the goddess of memory, for nine consecutive days and nights. The children of that ultra-marathon of love were the nine Muses. The Muses were the angels who blessed the efforts of poets, musicians, and dancers. As novelist Eliza Farnham (1815–1864) noted, "Each of the arts whose office is to refine, purify, adorn, embellish and grace life is under the patronage of a Muse."[84]

In a 2009 article in the *Wall Street Journal* entitled "Where Have All the Muses Gone?", cultural critic Lee Siegel describes the long history of creators relying on an invocation to the Muse, in one form or another. But, he notes, "Poets stopped invoking the muse centuries ago—eventually turning instead to caffeine, alcohol and amphetamines."[85]

Caffeine, alcohol, and amphetamines can help us shift out of our habitual, limiting mindsets, but overreliance on these substances damages our health and has diminishing returns. On the other hand, relying on an invocation to a creative source yields exponentially increasing benefits, without any negative side effects. Moreover, the Muses aren't just standing by to help artists; they're available for everyone who wants to bring more creativity to life. All you have to do is ask, wholeheartedly.

Qi Cultivation for Invoking the Muse

> When you bow deeply to the universe, it bows back.
> Morihei Ueshiba[86]

Bowing is an embodied way of invoking the Muse. It is a psychophysical expression of your openness to the creative universal energy. Humility is the soul of confidence and a surprising secret of creative genius. True inspiration comes from a source that is beyond the ego.

So, if it feels right to you, bow to the source of qi as you conceive it. Bow to the field of infinite potential, the divine, the Muses, or your higher self. The important thing is to gently efface the ego, leaving it at the threshold when you embrace a creative challenge.

Creators on Qi

Bill Douglas

Bill Douglas is the coauthor of *The Complete Idiot's Guide to T'ai Chi and QiGong* and the creative visionary who founded World Tai Chi &

Qigong Day, a global event involving mass exhibitions and teach-ins held annually in eighty nations. A 2009 inductee to the Internal Arts Hall of Fame in New York, Douglas is also an award-winning novelist. He believes that the arts of qi cultivation can promote creativity, health, and harmony on a global scale. He explains:

> For thousands of years these arts were the secrets of Chinese culture. In the last four decades they have expanded all across the planet at a time when most needed to help humanity. It is as though the fabric of creation has a creativity within it that has gestated this mind-body-spirit science for thousands of years in the womb of China and then released it into the world forty years ago, so that it would have time to permeate the globe and soak into local practitioners and position them to share it with the public—at a time when the planet would most require this elegant solution.[87]

What led Douglas to conceive and implement his big idea for World Tai Chi & Qigong Day? "As I surrendered to the field of qi through my own practice, I realized that I was connected to everything," he says. "This wasn't a religious belief, but rather something I experienced. This sense of connectedness and compassion is what inspired me to create this global event so that I could share this blessing with the world."[88]

On a personal level, Douglas's experience of qi transformed his life and unleashed his creativity:

> When I walked into my first tai chi class thirty years ago, I thought it was just another form of exercise like the ones I had grown up doing. I tried to make it hard, like isometrics, until one day my teacher walked over and put her hand on my shoulder, saying, "Bill, it's not supposed to be hard. If

it's hard, you are not doing it right. Let go. Breathe. Open. Loosen. Practice the art of letting go."

This became a metaphor for my life. The gentle motions of this ancient art became a way to untangle all my old traumas and limiting self-definitions. As I experienced qi flowing through my whole being, I started writing poetry. I took modern-dance classes and an improvisational acting class. My creativity blossomed.

The field of qi is the place from where all creativity springs. Many think that creativity is a linear construct, like a logic-based engineering project. But true creativity comes from the art of letting go. My books, DVDs, CDs, novels, and the concept that became World Tai Chi & Qigong Day—all these things were not things I worked out, but rather things that lilted into my consciousness when my mind had let go of everything. In their highest form, solutions are simple, elegant, and effortless.[89]

Q and A   Mastering the Creative Mindset

Q *Aren't we all affected by collective mindsets that can limit our individual creativity?*

A Yes. Some mindsets are personal and individual, while others are social or collective. In the United States collective mindsets about the abilities and rights of women, African-Americans, and homosexuals have, for example, undergone a major shift. It's only recently that the majority of citizens has been open to the possibility of a female CEO, a black president, or an openly gay person serving in the military.

Collective mindsets are harder to change than individual ones. Most of us were raised with a collective fixed mindset about our intellectual potential in general and our creative abilities in particular. That mindset, based on the neuroscience of the 1950s, was that your intelligence is fixed at age seven, that your brain degrades yearly after age thirty, and that your creativity, memory, and learning ability are fixed, can't be improved, and will inevitably decline with age. More recent research demonstrates that these assumptions are incorrect. We now know the following:

- Our mental abilities, including creativity, can improve throughout life. Neuroscientists call this *neuroplasticity.* (*Neuro* refers to neurons, otherwise known as brain cells, and *plasticity* is the quality of being changeable or malleable.)
- Although some brain cells die as we age, we can generate new cells. Neuroscientists call this *neurogenesis.*

Many people have a theoretical understanding of the notion of neuroplasticity, but they haven't integrated this new understanding into their personal mindset. Naming outdated beliefs that support a fixed mindset may make it easier to let go of those beliefs and shift to a creative mindset. I've coined two new words to help you understand the significance of the new, evolving paradigm (*paradigm* is another word for "collective mindset") and translate it into your personal mindset: *neurostatic* (static means "fixed") and *neuronecrotic* (*necrotic* from the Greek root *nekroun,* meaning "to make dead").

The neurostatic mindset was based on the belief that your mental potential was fixed at age seven and that there was nothing you could do to develop it. Neuroplasticity replaces neurostasis.

The neuronecrotic mindset was based on the belief that your brain cells inevitably degrade after age thirty, and that creativity and learning ability will therefore inevitably decline with age. Neurogenesis replaces neuronecrosis.

Q *So the creative mindset and the new paradigm of neuroplasticity are related?*

A Yes. As Carol Dweck emphasizes, "The brain has so much more plasticity than we ever dared to imagine. Even as adults we are generating new neurons, and that was never known before."[90]

We also now know that the more novelty and challenge involved in an activity, the greater will be the benefit for your brain. In part 3 you will be guided to experiment with new and, in some cases, challenging creative exercises. Practicing something you do not yet know how to do creates new neural connections and strengthens your brain. People with a fixed mindset don't want to do something new and challenging. The growth/creative mindset embraces novelty and challenge, thereby creating a positive spiral of progress and brain benefits.

Q *In addition to following the guidance in this section, what can I do to strengthen my creative mindset?*

A Embrace continuous learning. Surround yourself with people who support your growth orientation, who encourage your creative mindset. Seek positive role models, go out of your way to spend time with creative people, and study the lives of inspiring figures from history.

Q *How can I help my children avoid de-geniusing as they're growing up?*

A Combine unconditional love and encouragement with accurate, supportive performance feedback. Counter the dominance of the negative influences of contemporary social media and advertising by ensuring that your children get regular experiences of beauty and natural wonder. Most importantly, be a role model for the creative mindset. If your children observe you approaching difficulties with courage, playfulness, and confidence, they are much more likely to maintain those qualities as they face the challenges of growing up.

Q *How can I develop the self-awareness to notice when I'm caught in fixed-mindset patterns?*

A Regular qi cultivation will enhance your kinesthetic and energetic awareness, making it much easier for you to notice the physical and energetic patterns associated with fixed-mindset attitudes.

Q *I understand the importance of a creative mindset, but isn't talent important too?*

A Yes. Talent is a factor in achievement. If you're seeking your optimal path in life, it's best to discover the ideal confluence between your talents and your passion. Ken Robinson calls this finding your "Element." He writes, "Being in your Element is not only a question of natural aptitude. . . . Being in your Element needs something more—passion."[91]

Loving what you do is a key to happiness as well as the secret of high performance. In a classic study, A. D. de Groot (1914–2006), a Dutch researcher, found that the difference between chess masters and grandmasters could not be traced to any disparity in intellectual endowment. The distinguishing characteristic of the grandmasters was their love of the game. They played more, thought about it more frequently, and were more passionately involved in chess than the masters.[92] As grandmaster Raymond Keene, chess columnist of the *Times* of London and a former British champion, comments, "The key quality for success in chess is the love of the task that inspires determination."[93]

In other words, talent tends to be overrated as a predictor of long-term success. K. Anders Ericsson, a professor of psychology at Florida State University and author of *The Road to Excellence: The Acquisition of Expert Performance in the Arts and Sciences, Sports, and Games,* has devoted more than thirty years to studying the distinguishing characteristics of elite performers in disciplines ranging from chess and golf to surgery and singing. His comprehensive scientific inquiry yielded two conclusions:

1. Success in almost any discipline is more a function of training and practice than innate ability.
2. The most successful individuals in all areas of life, including creative endeavors, are distinguished by their disciplined, dedicated, and deliberate approach to practice.[94]

Q *What's the single most important aspect of the creative mindset?*

A The most important aspect of the creative mindset is the willingness to embrace the ambiguity and anxiety that you feel in the face of the unknown. One of my mottos is *"Anxietate tua semper prudenter utere"*—Latin for "Always use your anxiety creatively." Qi cultivation can help you transform the energy of anxiety into fuel for your creative fire.

Q *How do you apply the creative-mindset principles in your own life?*

A These principles are all drawn from my own practice over the past forty years. As an entrepreneur and sole proprietor, I re-create my business every year in alignment with my purpose. My business opportunities are a function of my clients' changing needs and whims, so confusion endurance, perseverance, and chutzpah are daily requirements. I nurture my sense of humor and play in many ways, including by watching comedy shows like *Seinfeld* or *The Big Bang Theory* before I go to sleep. I moved to Santa Fe, New Mexico, eight years ago so that I could be inspired by the beauty and wonder of nature every day. Most importantly, I invoke the Muse before every speech and seminar I lead and every time I sit down to write.

PART 3

MASTERING *the* CREATIVE PROCESS

If we are to achieve things never before accomplished,
we must employ methods never before attempted.

Francis Bacon (1561–1626), English philosopher[1]

E mbracing a creative mindset focuses your creative energy and liberates your potential for genius. Now you'll learn the different modes of thinking and the specific skills associated with the creative process. As you develop an understanding of the process and facility with the skills, you'll liberate even more creative energy.

You don't have to be a genius to learn how to think like one. Many people assume, mistakenly, that high IQ is a prerequisite for creativity, but the ability to be creative doesn't necessarily correlate with verbal or mathematical intelligence. There are plenty of folks with a high IQ who aren't particularly creative, and there are many very creative people who didn't get impressive scores on their SATs.

A few years ago I fulfilled one of my life dreams by attending a two-day program at the Porsche Sport Driving School in Alabama. It was an exhilarating and humbling experience. The professional drivers who gave the instructions attempted to show us how to get the most out of the magnificent machines. The most challenging task was learning how to shift gears at the right time to maximize the car's performance. By the end of the course, I realized that if I were driving a Carrera S and one of the instructors were driving the van that they used to bring us from our hotel to the track, I would still probably lose the race. In other words, the skill of the driver isn't necessarily correlated with the horsepower of the car.[2]

Whatever your intellectual horsepower, I will show you how to drive the creative process for better results in your life.

The Creative Process Requires Different Modes of Thinking

Mastering the creative process demands that we learn to shift between different modalities of thinking. The challenge is that most individuals and organizations have dominant modes they rely on and underdeveloped modes that they avoid. Abraham Maslow described the limitations of operating with only the habitual dominant mode: "I suppose it is tempting, if the only tool you have is a hammer, to treat everything as if it were a nail."[3] I follow Maslow with this caveat: if the man who only has a hammer treats everything as a nail, beware of the man who only has a screwdriver!

You can begin to assemble a balanced creative-thinking toolkit. The first step is to assess your own proclivities. Please read the statements below and note your immediate response to each one.

- I like to do research and collect data.
- I like to generate lots of ideas and think out of the box.
- I like to champion new ideas. I look on the bright side.
- I like to find flaws, liabilities, and weaknesses. I pride myself on my critical abilities.
- I like to pay attention to the emotions and feelings that are present when people are working on a creative challenge.
- I like to facilitate the process of shifting between different modes as appropriate.

- I like to spend lots of time in a relaxed, receptive mode.
- I like to make decisions. I enjoy taking on a complex problem and then making a clear decision about what to do.
- I like implementation. I prefer to be in the action mode.

Once you've read and reflected on each statement, please rank them according to your order of preference. For example, if your greatest preference among these options is to generate lots of ideas and think out of the box, then you will rank the second statement in first place. If the last thing you'd like to do is research and data collection, then rank the first statement in ninth place. Please create a rank order, even if it seems arbitrary, as it will provide a useful tool for understanding your strengths and weakness in the process of creation.

These nine statements reflect different modalities of thinking, all of which are necessary. Most people are strong in a few areas and weak in others. The same is true for work teams and corporate cultures. If you work on a team or are part of an organization, please take a few minutes and reflect on the relative strengths and weaknesses of your group in regard to these modalities. We will return to these nine modalities later; first let's explore the five phases of the creative process:

Preparation: Affirm your creative mindset. Define your creative challenge, examine preconceptions, and gather information.

Generation: Generate lots of ideas. Move beyond habitual pathways of thought.

Incubation: Sleep on it. Allow your intuition to suggest solutions.

Evaluation: Analyze and evaluate proposed solutions. Debate, then decide.

Implementation: Manifest your vision.[4]

Preparation: The Art of Seeing the Problem

It isn't that they can't see the solution.

It is that they can't see the problem.

G. K. Chesterton[5]

"You got a problem?"

When I was at high school in New Jersey, aspiring hoodlums in my class posed this question frequently. Maybe that's why I've always been interested in creative problem-solving.

When you formulate a problem thoughtfully, you are, as many great minds have advised, more than halfway toward a solution. In the Preparation Phase we aim to formulate the problem intelligently. This often involves redefining or reframing the initial question.

One of the classic examples of the power of question redefinition was provided by Peter Ueberroth, the organizer of the 1984 Summer Olympics in Los Angeles. The Olympics had been a money-losing proposition for decades. Previous organizers focused on how to lose less money. Ueberroth, who was influenced by creative-thinking pioneer Edward de Bono, PhD, MD, asked how the Olympics could become profitable while the aesthetic and inspirational elements of the games were improved. The result was an unprecedented success with a surplus of nearly $250 million, which was reinvested in youth sports-development programs throughout the United States. Ueberroth was named *TIME Magazine's* "Man of the Year" and awarded an honorary Olympic gold medal.

Another Olympic example of problem reframing led to a revolutionary approach to high jumping, the Fosbury Flop. Dick Fosbury, winner of the gold medal in 1968, effectively asked a simple question that changed the event forever: is there a better way (besides the variations of the straddle, scissor, or western roll techniques) to get over the bar? As he told *The Independent* newspaper in 2008, "My mind was driving my body to work out the best way to get over the bar." "Fearless Fosbury" was a twenty-one-year-old student of civil engineering when he invented the wildly unorthodox, head-first, back-to-the-bar method. Initially, his coaches thought he was crazy and warned that he would break his back. When he won the gold, they called him a genius. Forty years later, the Flop dominates global high-jump competition.[6]

In many problem-solving sessions, solutions become more apparent when the problem or question is reversed, redefined, or reframed.

Some problems are simple and clearly defined: What color was George Washington's white horse? What is eight times eight? These questions have just one answer. White was the color of Washington's white horse, and eight times eight will always be sixty-four. Much of our schooling focuses on solving these kinds of problems. We are trained to ask, "What is the right answer?"

More complex problems have many possible solutions and require a more creative approach. In the Preparation Phase instead of asking, "What's the right answer?" it is more constructive to ask, "Is this the right question?" and "What information do we need to intelligently begin our search for possible solutions or paths forward?"

Framing problems intelligently begins with reflection on your perspective. Captain Jack Sparrow (played by Johnny Depp) reminds us in *Pirates of the Caribbean,* "The problem is not the problem. The problem is your attitude to the problem. Do you understand?" Remember to affirm your creative mindset as you approach any problem.

Sometimes the most useful questions are the simple, naive questions that sophisticated people are prone to overlook: Why is this a problem? Why is it important? Is this the way we would do it if we weren't already doing it this way? How will we know that this problem has been solved? What problems might solving this problem cause? *And is this the real problem?*

Swersey, teacher of a popular class called "The Innovator's Studio" at Rensselaer Polytechnic Institute, is passionate about helping students excel in the Preparation Phase. An accomplished inventor and entrepreneur in his own right, Burt advises aspiring innovators, "The big step is problem-finding . . . finding and defining real problems."[7]

His most notable students were recently featured in the *New Yorker* magazine in an article describing their development of a technology for replacing plastics with an all-natural, environmentally friendly substance derived from mushrooms. When one of his students proposed a project to help grocery stores in India avoid the current necessity of disposing of food that had been handled by members of the untouchables caste, Swersey responded, "Find the real problem . . . Forget about the thrown-away food. Make it possible for the untouchables to be touchable."[8]

Swersey's advice touches the essence of the big problem with many problem-solving efforts: people often try to find solutions prematurely, before they've defined the real problem and collected sufficient data. And they often neglect to deliberately assess their potential biases. So in the Preparation Phase, it is essential to reflect on your prejudices.

Feelings play an intrinsic role in the search for creative ideas and solutions. Intuition, hunches, and gut feelings can be our most valuable allies. But our feelings can also lead us to be biased and blind to truth. Unmonitored, emotions determine our attitudes, setting the agenda for our perception and thinking.

Ultimately our actions are determined by emotion. We choose a particular course because, in the final analysis, it feels right. The key question is, when does our emotional judgment serve us best? Should we use it at the beginning, allowing our feelings to determine our perceptions and thoughts? Or should we try to allow our perception and thinking to operate objectively first, then follow our gut feelings after we've assembled sufficient information?

In order to separate feelings from analysis, we must first know what our feelings are. Ask yourself: How do I feel about this challenge? What are my real feelings about it? Do I have any prejudices, fears, or anxieties that prevent me from assessing this situation accurately?

If you are aware of your feelings, you have a much better chance to be objective. After decades of working with groups around the world, I've learned that people with advanced degrees and high levels of academic status tend to be less aware of their biases than others with less rigorous training. Scientists, physicians, and financial analysts, for example, often believe that because they have been trained to be objective, they are always objective and not driven by emotion. Their emotions are often repressed, operating in a shadow realm. Much of what passes for objectivity is a dangerous illusion predicated on repression of emotion.

We need to separate interpretation and opinion, both our own and that of others, from neutral consideration of data. Many people get stuck in the trap of looking only for information that confirms their prejudices. As psychologist and philosopher William James (1842–1910) observed, "A great many people think they are thinking when they are really rearranging their prejudices."[9]

Gather information: Ingredients for the Creative Recipe

If you want to cook something, the first thing you must do is assemble all the ingredients. Data, information, facts, observations, knowledge, and statistics form the basic ingredients for any creative recipe.

Sir Joshua Reynolds (1723–1792), founder of Britain's Royal Academy of Arts, observed, "Invention, strictly speaking, is little more than a new combination of those images which have been previously gathered and deposited in the memory; nothing can come from nothing."[10] Reynolds's observation applies to more than just painting. Creativity is all about making new connections and combinations. Therefore, it is important to begin with an inventory of that which has been "previously gathered and deposited in memory." In other words, do your best to assemble all the relevant facts and information before attempting to generate solutions.

Ask: What information do I need to understand this creative challenge? Where is it available? Who has experience with this sort of problem? Has someone already solved this?

When you've gathered the relevant information, considered your preconceptions, and explored different perspectives, then *create a written problem-statement or question.*[11] Articulate your problem or challenge as specifically as possible. Undefined, vague, or unclearly stated problems can seem out of reach, overwhelming, and insoluble. When you write out the problem, you begin marshaling your logical and intuitive resources to solve it. In the words of J. Krishnamurti, "If we can really understand the problem, the answer will come out of it, because the answer is not separate from the problem."[12]

Qi Cultivation for the Preparation Phase

The Preparation Phase demands that we gather information and suspend preconceptions so that we can define the real problem. Movement 2 of the Da Vinci Qi Practice, *Dimostrazione,* supports the ability to look at challenges openly and without prejudice.

Generation: The Art of Nonhabitual Thought

Genius, in truth, means little more than the faculty
of perceiving in an unhabitual way.
William James[13]

The word *generation* comes from the same Latin root as genius—*gignere*—meaning "to beget or produce." In the Generation Phase, we aim to beget or produce new ideas. This phase is what people usually are referring to when they talk about brainstorming.

As you generate lots of ideas, you create new patterns of association that invite the "Aha!" of insight. Generation disrupts automatic mental sets to liberate new possibilities. That sounds easy, but habitual patterns are doggedly persistent. Most people respond to the request "Associate freely" with a blank stare. Our reluctance to associate freely can be traced to our fear of embarrassment and of being judged by others.

Most of us invest tremendous energy in ensuring that we are never perceived as foolish, silly, or crazy. We internalize these fears so that even when alone we are unable to let our minds go free. In the Generation Phase, it is essential to allay the fear of judgment. To liberate new pathways required for insight, we must be willing to explore foolish, silly, and even seemingly crazy ideas.

Crazy people who are productive are geniuses. Crazy people who are rich are eccentric. Crazy people who are neither productive nor rich are just plain crazy. Geniuses and crazy people are both out in the middle of a deep ocean; geniuses swim, crazy people drown. Most of us are sitting safely on the shore. In the Generation Phase, you get your feet wet.

There are three elements to successful idea generation:

- Go for quantity.
- Suspend the expression of judgment.
- Have fun and seek the unfamiliar.

Go for Quantity

People who have many ideas are more likely to have creative ones.
Robert Ornstein, PhD, American psychologist and author[14]

If you've posed a well-framed question and are approaching it with a creative mindset, then you've established fertile ground for new ideas. If you throw one seed on that ground, your chances for new growth are slim. If you throw a hundred seeds, your chances improve. Throw a thousand, and you can expect a rich harvest.

The more ideas you generate, the greater your chances for a breakthrough. Thousands of silly, useless, and wrong ideas fertilize the blossoming of one really good idea. Generating lots of ideas pushes you outside habitual patterns and increases the possibility of making new connections, exponentially.

The strategy of generating lots of ideas has been employed and recommended by many great creative thinkers throughout history:

If you want to have good ideas you must have many ideas. Most of them will be wrong, and what you have to learn is which ones to throw away.

Linus Pauling (1901–1994),
biochemist and two-time Nobel laureate[15]

To have a great idea, have a lot of them.

Thomas Edison[16]

Look for an endless variety of things.

Leonardo da Vinci[17]

Ideas are like rabbits. You get a couple and learn how to handle them, and pretty soon you have a dozen.

John Steinbeck (1902–1969), American author[18]

If I have a thousand ideas and only one turns out to be good, I am satisfied.

Alfred Nobel (1833–1896), Swedish chemist and inventor[19]

Suspend the Expression of Judgment

A new idea is delicate. It can be killed by a sneer or a yawn; it can be stabbed to death by a quip and worried to death by a frown on the right man's brow.

Ovid (43 BCE–18 CE), Roman poet and playwright[20]

You will generate many more ideas if you temporarily suspend the expression of judgment. Most people understand the logic behind postponing evaluation, but nevertheless they proceed to mock others as soon as anything really different is expressed. Quips like, "When we asked for creative ideas, we didn't mean *that* creative," "What kind of weirdo are you, anyway?" and "Let's not waste our time on ridiculous speculation" have no place in the Generation Phase. Insidiously, many people express their hyperactive censor by aiming sneers and frowns at purveyors of off-the-wall ideas.

Friedrich Schiller observed, "In the case of the creative mind, it seems to me, the intellect has withdrawn its watchers from the gates, and the ideas rush in pell-mell, and only then does it review and inspect the multitude. You worthy critics, or whatever you may call yourselves, are ashamed or afraid of the momentary and passing madness which is found in all real creators, the longer or shorter duration of which distinguishes the thinking artist from the dreamer. Hence your complaints of unfruitfulness, for you reject too soon and discriminate too severely."[21]

Rejecting too soon and discriminating too severely are very common problems. People become impatient with the process, and anxiety rises as unfamiliar territory is explored. Whether expressed verbally or otherwise, criticism must be suspended in the Generation Phase. Remind yourself and others, if necessary, that criticism is essential, but that this is not the time for it. Emphasize that the task at hand is to act out a role that calls for the suspension of ordinary logic.

Asking people to act out a role is one of the most effective ways to get their creative juices flowing. The opportunity to play a role frees overly critical people from their habitual mode of thinking. Critics are often highly competitive, and if you inspire them to compete at generating lots of off-the-wall ideas, they will amaze you—and themselves.

One of the secrets of effective idea generation, for both individuals and groups, is to *exhaust habitual responses*. This won't happen if you don't suspend judgment. Push yourself into the unfamiliar. Usually, the best ideas in a generation session emerge toward the end, after people feel that they've shared everything they have to share.

Have Fun and Seek the Unfamiliar

In the Generation Phase, the more ideas the merrier, and the merrier the ideas the better. As we discussed in our consideration of the creative mindset, the *aha* of insight and the *ha-ha* of laughter are related intimately. Unfamiliar, absurd, and unusual ideas usually inspire laughter and move the mind outside of habitual pathways.

Sometimes the Generation Phase leads to an immediate breakthrough, an instant *aha* of insight and illumination. Frequently, however, it leads to an increased sense of chaos, confusion, and frustration. One of the most important things to understand is that the experience of increased uncertainty is a positive sign. If you have successfully shifted out of habitual perceptual and intellectual patterns, you may feel somewhat anxious. *The willingness to accept and embrace this inner tension is the key to using it creatively.*

It is much easier to face uncertainty with confidence if you understand that your mind has a faculty for translating your heightened state of unknowing into insights and solutions. This translation takes place in the Incubation Phase.

Qi Cultivation for the Generation Phase

The Inviting Genius Practice on page 48 is one of the most powerful ways to support the qi of the Generation Phase. But when it comes to generating new, creative ideas, it's best to have more than one approach. So I asked Stephen Russell, Barefoot Doctor, for his most powerful Generation Phase practice. Russell has been studying qi cultivation for more than forty-five years. In addition to his extraordinary gifts as a martial artist and healer, he is the author of sixteen books and many albums of exquisite healing music.

When I asked him about the relationship between qi and creativity, he explained, "To involve yourself in the creative process, to conjure something out of nothing, is an act of aligning yourself with qi, the generative force of existence. You render yourself a channel for this energy and the information that comes with it. Your role as an artist, no matter your field of expression, is to hone your ability to organize and express the inflowing energy and information in a form that will ultimately communicate the original pulse of creative energy to those whose lives may be enriched by it. In return, life will enrich you in many ways."[22]

He added, "Immersion in the creative process is its own reward. Any opportunities that may ensue as others find themselves drawn to your work and any financial gain derived by it are merely delightful bonuses."[23]

⚡ Barefoot Doctor's Prescription for Idea Generation

Sit or stand aligned around the vertical axis. Mindfully follow the flow of your breathing. Let go of any egocentric agenda and open your mind and heart to higher wisdom.

Inhale slowly and deeply, visualizing a fiber-optic-like beam of white light streaming from the point at the center of your forehead (the point of perception) up the midline of the forehead, backward over the midline of the skull, down the back of the skull, and into a point at the base of your skull (the Jade Pillow). Imbue this rear-ward flow with the pure essence of creativity.

As you exhale slowly and fully, visualize the beam of light streaming in the opposite direction and ultimately concentrating back to the point of perception. Imbue this forward flow with the pure essence of clarity.

Repeat the back-and-forth flow of breath and visualization nine times. Imagine yourself growing in creative sensitivity and mental clarity as you practice. Simultaneously visualize the entire crown area of your head becoming more open and receptive to a powerful, down-rushing stream of creative energy and information. Avoid analyzing the content of the information. Just imagine that you are an ultra-high-speed broadband connection pulling a stream of cosmic wisdom bits through your own energetic antenna.

Then simply let go, allowing your intuitive faculty to process what's been received. Wait patiently until the creative impulse gets so strong that you can't ignore it and you feel compelled to do your creative work.

Incubation: The Art of Doing Nothing

It takes a lot of time to be a genius.
You have to sit around so much, doing nothing, really doing nothing.
Gertrude Stein (1874–1946), American author[24]

When Leonardo da Vinci was painting *The Last Supper,* he worked fourteen hours at a time, for five or six days in a row. But then he'd disappear for a few days. This was very disturbing to the prior of the Church of Santa Maria delle Grazie, who had commissioned the painting. The prior didn't view Leonardo as history's greatest genius; rather, he saw him as just another contractor who wasn't paying attention to the completion deadline. The prior complained to the Duke of Milan, who had arranged the commission, and the duke summoned Leonardo and asked him to account for his absences. According to Giorgio Vasari (1511–1574), the first art historian, Leonardo explained, "Men of genius sometimes work best when they work least."[25]

Leonardo understood, intuitively, the importance of the Incubation Phase.

Upon reflection, most people recognize its importance. If you've ever solved a problem by sleeping on it, then you know what I mean.

Over the last thirty-five years I've asked thousands of people around the world this question: Where are you physically located when you get your best ideas? The most common answers are:

- In the shower
- Resting in bed
- Driving my car
- While walking or running (or doing other forms of exercise)
- At the beach

It's very rare for anyone to report getting their best ideas at work. What's going on in the shower, bed, or car that isn't happening in the workplace?

During the workday, we often experience pressure to conform and the fear of embarrassment, and our minds are in the active beta brainwave mode. In the shower, bed, or car, we relax; there's no fear of embarrassment and the mind shifts into slower alpha or theta waves, brainwave patterns that are conducive to creative insights.

If you've stimulated your mind through careful preparation and intense idea generation, you've set the stage for a breakthrough during incubation.

Unfortunately, many people run from one thing to another without leaving enough time for incubation. People spend hours in meetings without breaks and wonder why they aren't inspired. Give yourself a break and integrate breaks into your creative process. Work with intense focus and then relax and be receptive. As da Vinci counseled, "It is well that you should often leave work and take a little relaxation."[26]

The mathematical genius Henri Poincaré (1854–1912) called incubation "unconscious work" and described it this way: "Often when one works hard at a question, nothing good is accomplished at the first attack. Then one takes a rest . . . and sits down anew to the work . . . and then all of a sudden the decisive idea presents itself to the mind . . . These sudden inspirations never happen except after some days of voluntary effort which has appeared absolutely fruitless. These efforts have not been as sterile as one thinks; they have set agoing the unconscious mind."[27]

The Incubation Phase is most effective when we alternate, as Poincaré suggests, between periods of intense focus and rest. Without periods of intense focus, there is nothing to be incubated, nothing to set the unconscious mind agoing.

Discovering and learning to trust your incubatory rhythms makes the creative process more efficient and enjoyable. Years ago I discovered that I could trust these rhythms. In other words, when I studied hard and thought deeply about something, insights would arise more frequently and profoundly when I was relaxing, for example, in the shower, resting in bed, or enjoying a long walk. Eventually, I learned to *simply ask my intuitive mind to process a challenge and provide insights, and I discovered that this worked every time.* This process is built into the architecture of the mind.

Steven Pressfield expresses it beautifully: "What does it tell us about the architecture of our psyches that, without exerting effort or even thinking about it, some voice in our head pipes up to counsel us (and counsel us wisely) on how to do our work and live our lives? Whose voice is it? What software is grinding away, scanning gigabytes, while we . . . are otherwise occupied? Are these angels? Are they muses? Is this the Unconscious? The Self? Whatever it is, it's smarter than we are."[28]

As you learn to listen to the smarter part of yourself, you will become much more creative.

Songwriter Judy Collins explains it in simple terms: "When inspiration does not come, I go for a walk, go to the movies, talk to a friend, let go . . . The muse is bound to return again."[29] Comedic genius John Cleese adds, "This is the extraordinary thing about creativity: if just you keep your mind resting against the subject in a friendly but persistent way, sooner or later you will get a reward from your unconscious."[30]

But the reward from your unconscious is subtle and easy to overlook. In the Incubation Phase, we cultivate attention to delicate nuances of thought, listening for the faint whispers of shy inner voices.

These shy inner voices whisper to us through physical sensation. Every culture and language has equivalent phrases to the following English versions:

- I felt it in my gut.
- My blood whispered to me.
- I could feel it in my bones.
- I knew it in my heart.

The challenge is that your gut, blood, bones, and heart do not send memos, emails, or text messages. They speak to you when you relax—in the shower, for example. *So cultivate your creative reception by attuning to your proprioception.* As Conrad Hilton (1887–1979), creator of the world's first international hotel chain, comments, "I know when I have a problem and have done all I can to figure it out, I keep listening in a sort of inside silence, until something clicks and I feel a right answer."[31]

Relaxing and being receptive, listening in an "inside silence" for the "click" in your gut, blood, bones, and heart is a secret of sustaining the fire of genius. As you learn to appreciate and trust the power of incubation, you liberate tremendous creative energy. You will discover, as Leonardo da Vinci counsels, that you really do sometimes work best when you work least.

Qi Cultivation for the Incubation Phase

In order to be guided by "gut feelings," you must learn to feel your gut. Cultivating qi is the most efficient and effective way to enhance your creative reception by attuning to your proprioception. The Simple Standing Meditation and Simple Qi Walking Practice are particularly helpful in awakening you to the messages of your gut, blood, bones, and heart. The Central Channel Tune-Up and nourishing your qi are also valuable.

Creators on Qi

Jon Miller

Jon Miller is the former chairman and CEO of AOL and a very successful Internet entrepreneur and investor who has played a key role in creative projects such as Hulu, Kayak, and Tumblr.

What's the secret of Miller's creativity? He accesses the Incubation Phase using the power of qi. Miller explains:

> I have a specific technique that I use to bring more qi to the process of creative problem-solving. When I'm in the middle of a creative challenge and working intensively "in my head," I take a break and practice sitting meditation. I envisage the problem and, *without trying to solve it,* I sense the difference

between where we are and where we might want to be. In other words, I embrace the creative tension, the white space between the known and the unknown.

Then I do a qi-cultivation practice, usually a standing meditation, without thinking about the problem or trying to find an answer.

Next, I return to sitting meditation, focusing on the feeling of the enhanced flow of qi that was generated through the standing. At this point I can usually feel the movement of the qi through my central channel. I allow my attention to shift back to the problem, maintaining a receptive, open, and inquisitive attitude. This is when breakthrough thoughts seem to emerge spontaneously. Often, I experience a flow of many new ideas all at once.

Qi seems to prime the pump of my creative process, enlivening my intuition and elevating my creative energy. It works in a light, effortless, and natural way. Although I'm often dealing with issues that are quite serious and may have profound consequences for many people, I've learned to maintain a receptive, exploratory, and lighthearted approach in the midst of complexity.[32]

Evaluation: The Art of Hooking the Fish

Balancing preparation, generation, and incubation will move you beyond habitual ways of thinking, beckoning you to enter a world of unlimited possibilities. In the real world, however, some possibilities are clearly better than others.

Architect, inventor, and futurist Buckminster Fuller (1895–1983) referred to intuition as "cosmic fishing."[33] After baiting the hook through preparation and generation and trolling deep waters with incubation, you must now reel in the catch.

The first step in the Evaluation Phase is to organize and prioritize the ideas you have generated. Once you've put your ideas in order, subject them to cross-examination by playing the following roles: angel's advocate, devil's advocate, and judge.

Angel's Advocate

I dwell in Possibility
Emily Dickinson (1830–1886), American poet[34]

Speculative, optimistic thinking is the source of all accomplishment and an integral part of the creative process. In the angel's advocate role, focus on the bright side of the idea in question. Translate your idea into positive proposals and constructive suggestions. Engage in positive speculation, focusing on benefits and opportunities. Paint utopian scenarios and show how they can be realized. Express everything positive about the idea—all its strengths and the reasons it will work.

True positive thinking is a discipline. It is much easier to cut an idea down than to build one up, which is why it's best to play angel's advocate first.

Devil's Advocate

Rejection is the basis of logical thinking.
Edward de Bono[35]

Genuine creativity demands ruthless criticism. An effective devil's advocate acknowledges and suspends emotional reactions to an idea before pointing out reasons it will not work; weaknesses, gaps, and inadequacies; hazards, risks, and liabilities; everything that can possibly go wrong; consequences of failure; costs and difficulties of implementation; questionable data and unproven assumptions; potentially adverse legal and ethical implications; and faulty logic.

Thorough cross-examination by the devil's advocate may expose the weaknesses of an idea and inspire you to modify and strengthen it accordingly. It may send you back to the Preparation or Generation phases. Or it may confirm that you are on the right track and build confidence in your idea. You can be certain, however, that *if you don't play this role, then reality will do it for you.*

In the angel's advocate role, we imagine a better world and give the benefit of the doubt to optimism; in the devil's advocate role, we think in pessimistic terms, looking for everything that might go awry. We invoke the pragmatism of philosopher Niccolò Machiavelli (1469–1527), who noted, "How we live is so different from how we ought to live that he who studies what ought to be done rather than what is done will learn the way to his downfall rather than to his preservation."[36]

Judge

> Failures of perspective in decision-making . . . more often result
> from simple mistakes caused by inadequate thought.
> Herman Kahn (1922-1983),
> American futurist and founder of the Hudson Institute[37]

After your advocates have argued their cases, incubate again, and then appeal to your inner judge for deliberation. Comedian and author Tina Fey comments on the integration of the role of the judge and the Incubation Phase: "Sometimes if you have a difficult decision to make, just stall until the answer presents itself."[38] Consider:

Outcome—what is the idea supposed to achieve or accomplish?

Strengths—advantages of the proposed solution, benefits, summary of angel's advocate case.

Weaknesses—disadvantages of the idea, costs, summary of devil's advocate case.

Interesting—aspects of the idea and its possible consequences that are neither positive nor negative, but just interesting.

Audience—who is the audience, client, or customer for your idea?

Success—what are your criteria for success and failure, and how will you know that you have succeeded?

After you consider every aspect of the proposed solution, it is time to decide. Ultimately, our decisions are influenced by our values, and our values are deeply laden with emotion. Having held your feelings in abeyance to map your thoughts objectively, this is the time to bring them forth. The essence of effective decision-making is to *integrate all relevant information and then trust your gut.*

Successful people in all walks of life are ultimately guided by their intuitive wisdom. Weston Agor, author of *The Logic of Intuitive Decision Making,* discovered through extensive interviews that top executives are distinguished by their ability to use intuition effectively in making important decisions.[39] Basketball genius LeBron James reports that when he asked Warren Buffett for guidance, Buffet told him, "[A]lways follow your gut. When you have that gut feeling, you have to go with it."[40]

In 1960, Ray Kroc's lawyers advised him against spending nearly $3 million on a couple of burger joints and the rights to the McDonald's name. Kroc (1902–1984) said that his "funny bone" told him to over-rule his counsel and make the deal.[41]

How can you learn to trust your funny bone?

Eugene Gendlin, PhD, author of *Focusing,* developed one of the best tools for checking the reliability of your funny bone. He calls it "instant hindsight." Gendlin advises you to affirm your intuition and then attune to any bodily sensations that either confirm it or call it into question.[42] In other words, say, as though you really mean it, something like, "The issue is resolved. My intuition or decision feels right. I feel good about it. *N'est-ce pas?* (French for 'Isn't it so?')" Then attend carefully to the bodily sensations that arise as you question the wisdom of your intuition. If the sensations are queasy, then you may be off the mark; if the feelings are more pleasant, then you are probably on course.

Qi Cultivation for the Evaluation Phase

You can access the energy that supports the angel's advocate, devil's advocate, and judge with these simple but very powerful standing postures.

⚡ Three Stances for Evaluation

Angel's Advocate Stance: Begin in a wide version of the basic
standing posture. With a lengthening spine, sink your body gently
toward the ground by bending your knees as far as is comfortable. Reach your hands down toward the earth, scooping up earth
energy, and then draw your hands up along the right and left channels respectively, as though you were offering the earth energy
up to the sky. Finish with your knees bent and your hands at face
level, palms toward your face, with fingers branching up to the sky

figure 3.1 The Angel's Advocate Stance   **figure 3.2** The Devil's Advocate Stance

(figure 3.1). Gaze up beyond your fingertips toward the sky. The feeling is like that of a tree growing up toward the sun. Also known as Maximum Yang Stance, this is an ideal posture for aligning with the positive, optimistic viewpoint required by the angel's advocate. Enjoy the posture for thirty seconds to one minute.

Devil's Advocate Stance: Begin in the basic standing posture. Turn your left foot and then your right foot inward so that you are standing pigeon-toed. Let your arms float up to make a diamond shape; the elbows point away from the torso, while the palms face down. Squeeze your fingers together so that there's no space between them, and point your fingertips toward one another at the level of your navel. (See figure 3.2.) The feeling in this posture, also known as Maximum Yin Stance, is the protection of vulnerability. In the devil's advocate role, you protect the integrity of your creative process by considering the potential weaknesses and vulnerabilities inherent in your ideas, and this stance is conducive to that awareness. Hold the posture for thirty seconds to one minute.

Judge's Stance: Begin in the basic standing posture. As you exhale, let your body sink down slightly by bending your knees as your arms float up to create a diamond shape in front of you, with your fingertips at the level of your navel, palms facing down (figure 3.3). This diamond

figure 3.3 The Judge's Stance

147

shape is softer and less defined than the one in the Devil's Advocate Stance. Feel the air in between your fingers and keep your
attention on the negative space around you. Rest in this ancient
posture of balanced neutrality for thirty seconds to one minute.

Creators on Qi

Jim Alexander

Jim Alexander is an attorney who began practicing qi cultivation
about twenty years ago. He writes, "My profession tends to be
populated with overly aggressive and egotistical practitioners.
Before I began training my qi, I confess that I was one of them."[43]

Alexander has discovered that awareness of qi helps him be more
centered and better able to read the energy of both clients and
adversaries. He explains:

> The mythology surrounding the legal profession makes most
> people distrustful of their own attorney. I've learned that
> rather than pushing through someone's defenses, I can shift
> into a receptive state. This not only puts my clients at ease,
> but it also results in much deeper intuitive insight into their
> cases. Clients are often surprised and frequently respond,
> "Why did you ask that question? How did you know?" I
> am convinced these creative insights are more than just a
> reflection of my years of experience, but also a direct result
> of my sensitivity to the flow of qi. How can I be sure it is qi
> that promotes creative insights? Because I can feel it when it
> is happening. On those days when I don't do my qi practice,
> I'm just not as creative.[44]

I asked Alexander to share an example of how his awareness of qi helps
him in the adversarial situations that he encounters. He responded,

The ability to be centered, to feel the flow of energy through my central channel, helps me avoid being reactive and making situations worse. Instead, I've learned to listen and draw in the qi, for example, of a hostile witness. On one memorable occasion I was taking an opponent's deposition. Depositions are sworn statements recorded by a court reporter with opposing attorneys present. On this occasion the deponent was well prepared. He bristled with aggression while waiting for the interrogations to begin. Before I began, I sat in meditation (with my eyes open), breathing into my lower center, and silently absorbed his aggressive energy. Then the path forward became clear, and I said, "I am prepared to be here all afternoon, but if you want to please tell in your own words what happened, then we will be done." He did. Five minutes later, the deposition and case were over. Any first-year law student will tell you my question was amateurish and likely to be ineffective, yet I was absolutely confident of its results. Why? Because it was obvious to me that his aggression was masking a weak center and that he would respond to a firm, positive suggestion.

Alexander adds, "When qi flows harmoniously, insights just seem to happen. The result is that I'm more effective, more creative, and it's made my profession much more fun."[45]

Implementation: The Art of Getting It Done

> Every one who has taken a shower has had an idea.
> It's the person who gets out of the shower, dries off and does something about it that makes a difference.
> Nolan Bushnell, American entrepreneur[46]

In school we are usually asked to solve problems that are:

- well defined and formulated by others,
- accompanied by a source of information necessary to solve the problem (a text, for example),
- solved with just one correct answer,
- not related to our life experience.

In life we usually must solve problems that are:

- not predefined and self-formulated;
- not accompanied by a source of information necessary to solve the problem;
- solved by a multiplicity of potential answers, each associated with different benefits and costs;
- relevant to our everyday experience.

The bulleted lists above are adapted from an article by Richard K. Wagner entitled "Smart People Doing Dumb Things: The Case of Managerial Incompetence."[47]

The main reason that academically smart people may have trouble solving real-life problems is a lack of what psychologist Robert Sternberg and his colleagues call "practical intelligence." Sternberg et al. have defined three complementary intelligences that we need to drive the creative process.[48]

Synthetic intelligence is what most people refer to when they think of creativity. It's the primary intelligence needed in the Generation and Incubation phases.

Analytic intelligence is what most people think of as the force behind critical thinking. It's the key to the Preparation and Evaluation phases. In the creative process, critical thinking is just as important as synthetic thinking. The secret is to apply it at the right time.

Practical intelligence isn't usually associated with creativity, but without implementation we are, as poet and philosopher Henry David Thoreau (1817–1862) suggested, just "building castles in the air." Thoreau advises that we "put the foundations under them."[49] Practical intelligence is the art of foundation building. It is the ability to do what needs to be done in a particular context in order to achieve an objective. It is required to champion an idea, generate buy-in, overcome obstacles, sell the idea, and translate it into reality.

Sternberg and his colleagues have demonstrated that there's no necessary correlation between academic success and practical problem-solving. Bennett Goodspeed (1938–1983), founder of the consulting firm Inferential Focus, commented on the failure of academic training to instill practical intelligence when he noted, "If Thomas Edison had an MBA, he would have tried to invent a bigger candle."[50]

It's not just the analytically intelligent who may lack implementation skills; many people who possess a high degree of synthetic intelligence also do not have the wherewithal to translate their creative ideas into reality.

For both MBAs and artists, practical intelligence is the key to the Implementation Phase. Successful creators know that writing the novel or script, painting the masterpiece, designing the app, developing the new marketing campaign, composing the song, or writing the entrepreneurial business plan *is the easy part of the process.* The hard part is getting funding, building alliances, overcoming obstacles, resolving conflicts, getting more funding, generating buy-in, publicizing and selling what you've created. As philosopher and mathematician A. N. Whitehead (1861–1947) emphasizes, "Ideas won't keep. Something must be done about them."[51]

The Implementation Phase is when you set goals, make plans (and prepare to improvise), and then commit to the realization of your vision.

In a recent article, J. Robert Baum, director of Entrepreneurship Research at the University of Maryland, explains, "General intelligence is not enough. Practical intelligence can mean the difference between entrepreneurial success or failure." Baum defines practical intelligence as "an experience-based accumulation of skills and explicit knowledge as well as the ability to apply that knowledge to solve everyday problems."[52] In other words, it's know-how or ingenuity.

If you're interested in ingenuity, in achieving your most important goals, then there's probably no better role model than Thomas Edison.

Edison had exceptional synthetic intelligence. His ability to generate ideas amazed his coworkers. Edison also had outstanding analytical and critical abilities. He played the role of ruthless devil's advocate on every aspect of all his products before they ever were presented to the public. But what makes Edison a uniquely valuable role model is his unprecedented combination of synthetic, analytic, and practical intelligences.

Thomas Edison didn't just invent the light bulb; he developed a system for lighting the entire world. He also invented the phonograph and much of the technology for the development of moving pictures, thereby launching the modern entertainment industry. Edison generated a record 1,093 US patents, but his greatest invention of all was never patented. Edison's greatest invention was the creation of a systematic approach to innovation that he called his "invention factory."[53] He pioneered the practice of research and development and linked it with commercialization through production, marketing, and sales. He shared his ideas on success in his voluminous notebooks and in many interviews with the media.

His approach to goal-setting and manifestation offers a profound example of practical intelligence. You can access and apply the same principles that he did; to get started, consider this new spin on a simple acronym that expresses essential elements of effective goal-setting: SMART.

S   **Specific.** Define what you want to accomplish in detail.

M   **Measurable.** Determine the criteria you will use to measure your achievement.

A   **Accountable.** Assume full responsibility for achieving your goal. (The common version of this acronym has the A stand for "achievable." I've thrown that out because most people don't set unachievable goals, but they do often neglect to take full responsibility for achieving the goals they've set.)

R   **Relevant.** Ensure that your goals are relevant to your overall purpose and values. (The common version of this acronym has the R stand for "realistic." I've thrown that out for the same reason I've deleted "achievable." Most people don't set goals that are unrealistic, but they do often set goals that aren't aligned with their purpose and values.)

T **Timeline.** Write down the exact date that you will achieve your goal, and specify milestones along the way. Without a clear timeline, you are just fantasizing rather than goal-setting.

Despite the clever acronym, people often forget to apply this system for setting goals and implementing plans. Why? For your brain to remember to organize behavior in alignment with a goal, it must connect the energetic component with its rational component. In other words, many goals remain unfulfilled because they're not aligned with your passions. Understanding how to set goals so that they will be remembered and translated into behavior is an essential key to mastering the creative process.

How do you integrate the emotional and rational elements in goal-setting? The secret is to invoke a second acronym: EDISON.[54]

E **Energy.** Express your goal in terms that energize you.

D **Decision.** Be decisive about what you intend to manifest. Make a committed decision even if you can't see the path forward to the realization of your goal.

I **Integration.** Consider how each goal you set will be integrated with your other goals and your overall purpose.

S **Sensory.** Use all your senses to vividly imagine the achievement of your goal.

O **Optimistic.** Without optimism there is no creativity or innovation.

N **Now.** Begin it now!

Take one of your goals and consider it from a SMART EDISON perspective. If you apply the ideas in the entire two-part acronym, you will discover that you begin to get better results. Many people are amazed by the power of this simple process. As Edison observed, "If we all did the things we are capable of doing, we would literally astound ourselves."[55]

In addition to SMART EDISON goal-setting, sales, negotiation, presentation, and leadership skills are essential components of the Implementation Phase that can all be developed with appropriate training and deliberate practice.

Qi Cultivation for the Implementation Phase

We all know people whose heads are in the clouds. They dream wonderful dreams but have trouble implementing them. Other folks are so busy executing practical tasks that they lose touch with their dreams. The creative process demands that we find a balance between our dreams and our reality, our ideals and their implementation. In ancient tradition, finding this balance is known as bridging heaven and earth. Here's a simple, practical way to experience this integration energetically.

⚡ Bridging Heaven and Earth

From the basic standing posture, inhale and press your left hand down toward the outside of your left foot. Connect to the energy of the earth through the heart of your left palm. Turn your head left to watch the hand as it presses down.

While maintaining the earth connection with your left hand, exhale and extend your right hand up to the sky, allowing it to spiral up so that at full extension it is as though you are balancing a tray on your right hand. Turn your head upward and watch the right hand as it rises, connecting to the energy of the sky through the heart of your right palm. Your arms are now stretching vertically in opposite directions. (See figure 3.4.)

Hold your breath as you move both hands to your lower center and consolidate the energies of earth and sky there.

Now inhale and press your right hand down toward the outside of your right foot. Connect to the energy of the earth through the heart of your right palm and watch the hand as it presses down. While maintaining the earth connection of your right hand, exhale and extend your left hand up to the sky. Watch the left hand as it spirals up, connecting to the energy of the sky through the heart of your left palm.

Hold your breath as you return your hands to your lower center and consolidate the energy of earth and sky there. You have just finished one cycle.

Repeat the movements for seven complete cycles.

As you reach toward the earth, you connect with the grounded energy you need to get things done and overcome obstacles. As you reach to the sky, you connect with the celestial energy you'll need to maintain the vision of your goal. When you hold your breath and bring earth and sky together at your lower center, you are integrating the visionary and grounded energies required to translate your creative idea into reality.

figure 3.4 Bridging Heaven and Earth

Nine Hats for the Five Phases

The *Cambridge University Dictionary* defines the phrase "put your thinking cap on" as "to think seriously about something." Thanks to Edward de Bono, we know that there are different types of thinking that require different cap styles. He introduced the idea of shifting between different-colored thinking caps in order to free ourselves from habitual thinking modes. De Bono's pioneering work as a cognitive milliner led to his suggestion for the following chapeaux:

The **white hat.** White represents purity. The white hat is the mode for a purely objective focus on collecting data. Put on the white hat when you want to gather information—for example, in the Preparation Phase.

The **green hat.** Green is the color of growth and springtime. Put on the green hat and let your ideas grow and flourish. This is the primary hat in the Generation Phase. It's open to unlimited possibilities and alternatives.

The **yellow hat.** Yellow represents the sun that shines brightly on all ideas. Put on the yellow hat and look for the benefits and strengths of an idea. This is the hat worn by the angel's advocate.

The **black hat.** The black hat is the headgear of the devil's advocate. Put this on to consider liabilities, weaknesses, costs, and all possible negative implications of an idea.

The **red hat.** Red represents emotion. Put on the red hat and tune into your feelings and intuitions. When you wear this hat, you can express emotions and share likes and dislikes without having to justify them. Keep the red hat handy in all phases so that you can distinguish your feelings from your rationality.

The **blue hat.** Blue represents the clarity of the open sky. It's for thinking about thinking. This is the hat for the facilitator role. Put on the blue hat to monitor transitions between the phases and the hats.[56]

I've complemented de Bono's six hats with three more:

The **sleeping cap** is worn in the Incubation Phase. Put on the sleeping cap when you want to allow your ideas to percolate.
The **judge's wig** is worn when you must make a decision.
The **hard hat** is worn in the Implementation Phase. Put on the hard hat when you must focus on getting things done. You can inscribe this motto, from British poet and visual artist William Blake (1757–1827), on your hard hat: "He who desires, but acts not, breeds pestilence."[57]

The nine hats correspond to the nine modalities introduced at the beginning of part 3, in "The Creative Process Requires Different Modes of Thinking."

You can use the five phases and nine hats on your own. They are particularly valuable when you are working with others because they make it easier for people to become aware of their habitual, default thinking modalities. And that heightened awareness makes it easier for people to change.

Qi Cultivation for Shifting between the Phases, Hats, and Intelligences

Creativity requires us to shift appropriately between different phases of the creative process and different ways of thinking. You can support your ability to move from one mode to another intellectually by cultivating the ability to change modes kinesthetically and energetically. Many traditional qi-cultivation practices focus on moving seamlessly between an active and a more receptive state, and from one elemental quality to another.

I was introduced to this Shifting Modes Practice many years ago when Chungliang Al Huang led a version of it for a large group at a conference where we shared the podium. It immediately elevated and harmonized the energy of the whole group. Since that time, I've led this for many large groups around the world, and it always works. You can also get the benefits just doing it on your own.

⚡ Shifting Modes Practice

As you shift your body and move your energy, you become more attuned to the right intelligence or right hat in the right place at the right time. Moving in a rhythmic, harmonious, and graceful way will help you become more receptive to the rhythm, harmony, and grace of the creative energy.

You'll get the most from this practice by being especially mindful of the moments of transition. As you move between expansion and contraction, one side and the other, and from earth to fire to air to water, you are sending a message to your psyche to be ready to shift modes as life requires.

You can do the five parts in the sequence presented, as a single practice, or experiment with any order that appeals to you. You can do them all in one practice session, or just one or two, as the spirit moves you.

Part 1: Weight Shifting

Begin in the basic standing posture. Allowing your knees to bend comfortably, shift your weight 100 percent to your left foot and then 100 percent to your right. Continue shifting your weight rhythmically. The key is to maintain alignment around your vertical axis as you shift; in other words, avoid flopping around. Keep the soles of your feet in full contact with the ground throughout the movement. As you find a nice rhythm, you'll discover that this movement is very soothing for your nervous system. Enjoy the weight-shifting practice for a minute or two and then pause. Feel the enhanced flow of qi throughout your whole being.

Part 2: Drawing Up Earth Energy

Widen your stance as far as is comfortable and smile. Sink your energy through the Bubbling Spring points deep into the earth, even as your apex points up to the sky.

Turn your feet so that you can easily turn your body to the left about 45 degrees. Keep your feet parallel, and after you've moved to the left, maintain both feet in full contact with the ground. With a lengthening spine, bend your left knee so that you can easily reach toward your left foot with both hands to gather the energy of the earth (figure 3.5). Pull the energy up from the ground as you straighten up and your hands move up along either side of your left leg. Reach down a second time, even more deeply into the earth, and draw the energy back up through your leg and into your lower center.

figure 3.5 Gathering qi from the earth

Then shift your feet and torso toward your right at a 45-degree angle. With a lengthening spine, bend your right knee so that you can easily reach toward your right foot with both hands to gather the energy of the earth. Pull the energy up from the ground as you straighten up and your hands move up along either side of your right leg. Reach down a second time, even more deeply into the earth, and draw the energy back up through your leg and into your lower center.

Repeat this movement three to five times on each side. Bring special attention to the transition between sides. As you shift from side to side, you may feel a pleasant sense of fullness between your hands. Enjoy the feeling of gathering and storing the qi of the earth.

Part 3: Playing with Fire Energy

From the basic standing posture, with feet shoulder width apart, shift your left leg forward and right leg back. Place your right foot at a comfortable angle between 15 and 45 degrees. The distance from the back heel of your front foot to the front of your back foot should be at least the same as the width

figure 3.6 For part 3 of the Shifting Modes Practice, "Playing with Fire Energy," the arms swing forward as the weight shifts toward the front of the feet. As the weight shifts back, the arms pull back, and the hands form fists.

of your shoulders, or more, as is comfortable. Your weight is evenly distributed between both feet.

Maintaining your alignment around the vertical axis, and keeping the soles of your feet in contact with the ground, begin shifting your weight forward and back. As you move forward, let your arms extend straight out in front of you with palms facing down and fingers stretching out toward the horizon (figure 3.6). As you move back, draw in your arms, as though you were rowing. As you shift your weight back, your hands close into soft fists next to their respective hip creases (figure 3.7). As you move forward and extend your arms, let your eyes get fiery (without anger) and make a sharp, cutting *saaah* sound.

Continue for one minute, accelerating the pace and intensity with each movement forward and back.

Return to the basic standing posture, and then shift your right leg forward and your left leg back. Repeat the movements on the other side. Continue for one minute, accelerating the pace and intensity with each movement forward and back.

Part 4: Dancing with Air Energy

From the basic standing posture, come up onto your toes and let both arms float up above your head.

figure 3.7 For part 3 of the Shifting Modes Practice, "Playing with Fire Energy," the arms swing forward as the weight shifts toward the front of the feet. As the weight shifts back, the arms pull back, and the hands form fists.

Wiggle your fingers and feel the air between them. Imagine that your whole body is just drifting and floating on air currents. Your eyes look heavenward, and the feeling is as though you are being carried away. Enjoy this dancelike movement for thirty seconds. If you like, you can have even more fun by making the sound of the wind blowing through aspen trees as you float.

Part 5: Calming with Water Energy

From the basic standing posture, move your feet a little bit wider apart. Place both of your hands in front of the lower center about an inch or two in front of your body, with the palms facing one another to begin. As gently, slowly, and smoothly as you can, move your hands apart as though you are calming the surface of water. Your palms will slowly shift so that they are facing down as you move your arms out to the sides as far as is comfortable. Inhale as you move your hands out and exhale as you bring them back to center, slowly returning to the starting position. As you exhale, enjoy an extended, soothing *ahhhh* sound. Repeat eight times.

However many parts you choose to do, finish your practice by nourishing your qi.

Al Huang comments, "By playing with these exercises, you learn to adapt, change, and transform in harmony with nature and thus discover your true nature. Use the structure of the exercises as a basis, but don't be confined by them. Just as a jazz musician improvises with a melodic line, you too can improvise. The living dance of life is much more important than the notes of the prescribed routine. Consider the movements as prompts for creative experimentation and play."

He adds, "Qi is the breath of life, the link to our ineffable origin; as we play and dance with it, we connect to our spirit. It manifests in the sky, in the open space of the cosmos, and through the earth we live on and come from and return to when we die. From the first breath of your life to the last, you are living this dance of 'shifting modalities.'

"The circular, rhythmic flow of seeming opposites—inhale and exhale, earth and sky, water and fire, yin and yang—is always with you. There is no division. Dance on!"[58]

Bill Gallen

Bill Gallen has been practicing and teaching qigong and tai chi for more than thirty years. He's also a gifted and accomplished landscape painter and a renowned art teacher. Gallen says, "Qi is the animating energy of life. It is the aliveness of the world and is found in all manifestations of creation. Qi is the ocean, creativity the ship."[59]

He adds, "As a painter I'm drawn where aliveness is apparent. Although they are static material objects, the best paintings are streaming with energy. The *Tai Chi Classics* describe this as 'stillness in motion.' Or as Gene Wilder exclaimed in *Young Frankenstein:* 'Its alive!'"[60]

Gallen emphasizes the importance of the interplay of active and receptive modes in his creative work. He explains:

> A great work requires the sublime marriage of yin and yang, receptive and active. Listening, observing, and contemplating belong to the receptive mode. Out of perception and preparation come possibility. In the pursuit of mastery, this is the pregnancy that lasts for ten thousand hours. Action, painting, is the grace arising from this patient process.
>
> Then, of course, one must deal with the gallery and the business side of work. All the phases must be studied assiduously with special attention to the harmonious flow from one to another. Creative action will always be predicated on pregnant preparation. It's a question of balance. For myself, and for many of my students, cultivating qi is the best way to hone the sensitivity to this balance.[61]

Mind Mapping: Multipurpose
Creative-Process Tool[62]

If I were to recommend just one method for mastering the creative process, it would be Mind Mapping. Often called the "Swiss Army Knife of the mind," Mind Mapping is a versatile tool for generating and organizing ideas using images and key words in a nonlinear format. Originated by English author and poet Tony Buzan, Mind Mapping enhances all five phases of the creative process.

How to Mind Map

It's best to make a Mind Map on a large piece of blank paper and to use many different colored pens, but you can also do it on a small notepad with just one pen if necessary. Although there are many software programs available for Mind Mapping, *it's much better to learn to do it by hand before using the computer.* When you draw your own creative doodles and print your own key words by hand, you stimulate your brain in a way that is much more engaging than clicking on someone else's icon and dragging it.

Put a symbol or a picture representing your problem/creative challenge at the center of your page. Starting at the center rather than at the top of the page helps to free you from the limitations of hierarchical, top-down thinking. It opens your mind to a full 360 degrees of association. Pictures and symbols are easier to remember than words, and enhance your ability to think creatively about your subject. Your drawing will serve as the home base for your creative associations.

Print key words on lines radiating from your central image. Key words are the information-rich nuggets of creative association. They are easier to remember than sentences or phrases and can be generated more quickly, without sacrificing meaning. Moreover, training yourself to look for key words enhances your ability to get to the essence of your problem. Printing is easier to read and remember than cursive. By linking words with lines, you'll show clearly how one key word relates to another. Connect the lines for maximum clarity.

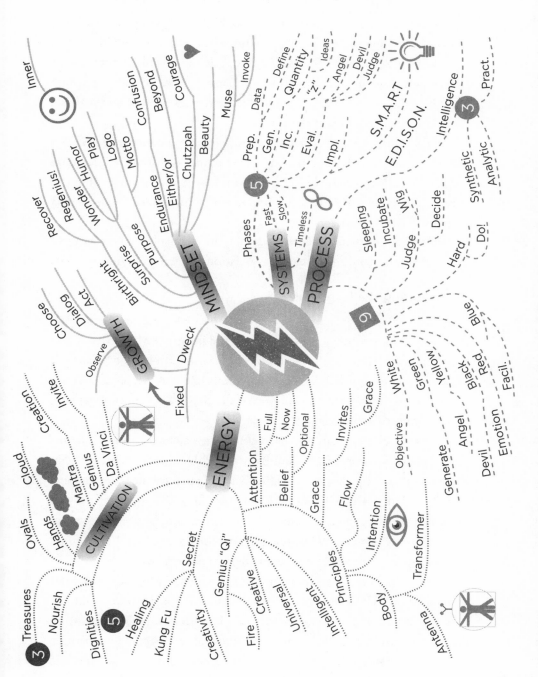

figure 3.8 A sample Mind Map of *Creativity on Demand*

165

Print one key word per line and make the length of the word the same as the length of the line it is on. Placing just one word per line trains you to focus on the most appropriate key word, enhancing the precision of your thought and minimizing clutter. Making the length of the word and the line it is on the same size saves space and makes it easier to view your ideas at a glance.

Add colors and pictures. Colors and pictures enhance memorability and imagination. Emphasize important points and show relationships between different branches of your Mind Map with color-coding (for example, yellow for the most important points, blue for secondary points, and so forth).

Draw pictures and images, preferably in vivid color, wherever possible; they stimulate your creative association and enhance your memory.

Facilitating the Five Phases

In the Preparation Phase, use Mind Mapping to capture all relevant information. Because it uses key words and images, a Mind Map allows you to display a tremendous amount of information in an efficient way, and it makes it easier to discover connections. A problem well formulated is almost solved, and one of the best ways to formulate your problem is to Mind Map it.

In many cases, an initial problem-definition map leads to immediate and unexpected solutions. As Madhu Jayawant, PhD, a former research fellow from DuPont, explains, "I used Mind Mapping to integrate a large amount of apparently unrelated data on a pulp-bleaching process. I put the data on a Mind Map, and as I began to make connections between the various elements of the process, I identified and defined an invention." The process took him less than one hour and resulted in a patentable discovery.[63]

Mind Mapping is a powerful tool for generating lots of ideas. Starting with a picture or symbol jump-starts the imagination, while the branching format encourages free association. Traditional brainstorming sessions often result in a high volume of disconnected ideas written on Post-it notes or flip charts. By printing key words, one per line, and keeping the lines connected, Mind Mapping helps you track and build upon the flow of ideas in the Generation Phase.

If you run out of ideas for your Mind Map, pause, take a deep breath, and then print random words to open up new pathways. You can also take any key word on your map and draw three blank lines radiating from it. The mind's natural tendency to complete a gestalt will inspire you to fill the lines with new associations.

Brainstormers often find that they must first burst out all their standard thoughts and habitual responses before discovering new pathways. Mind Mapping makes this happen more quickly and enjoyably.

Mind Mapping can also make the Incubation Phase more fruitful. When you draw pictures and use colors to represent your ideas, you are recruiting the more imaginative parts of the mind into the problem-solving process. This provides more stimulus and inspiration for the unconscious, underground work that takes place when we "sleep on it."

In the Evaluation Phase, Mind Mapping makes it easier to summarize both the angel's advocate and devil's advocate positions, thereby making the work of the judge simpler. And in the Implementation Phase, the Mind Map makes it easier to generate and visualize the plan. In a group setting, Mind Mapping's visual nature makes it much easier for everyone to have a shared vision of the implementation strategy.

Overcoming Premature Organization

For most people, the biggest block to the creative process is *premature organization*. The school-bred fear of mistakes and embarrassment leads many individuals to attempt to put their ideas in order and analyze them before devoting sufficient time and energy to generating new ideas. This syndrome is exacerbated when we are taught outlining and other linear note-taking methods.

Outlining is valuable as a tool for presenting ideas in a formal, orderly fashion after the real thinking has been done. If you try to generate your ideas in a top-down, linear fashion you will find that it slows you down and stifles your freedom of thought. It is just plain illogical to try to organize your ideas before you've generated them. Many people understand this notion theoretically but remain stuck in a linear framework that limits their creative-thinking ability.

Mind Mapping frees you from the tyranny of premature organization. It helps you access and balance the three intelligences so that you can use all your creative power.

The cure for premature organization is to *generate first, then organize.* It's like the writer's motto: write drunk, revise sober. If you write sober and revise sober, your work is boring and no one wants to read it. If you write drunk and revise drunk, no one *can* read it. Write drunk (generate lots of ideas), then revise sober (organize and analyze your ideas).

Some folks naturally generate lots of ideas in a flowing, nonlinear fashion, but never bother to organize them. And others generate and organize but never get around to implementation. Mind Mapping helps liberate the generation mode and makes it easier to organize ideas because you can see the relationships between them more readily. It makes your implementation plan more memorable and inspiring.

Balancing Two Systems of Thinking: Fast and Slow

> If I had one wish, it is to see organizations dedicating some effort
> to study their own decision processes and their own mistakes,
> and to keep track so as to learn from those mistakes.
> Daniel Kahneman, Nobel laureate in Economics[64]

Unlike car racing, where one attempts to go as fast as possible all the time, thinking requires different speeds to stay on track. In *Thinking, Fast and Slow,* Nobel laureate Daniel Kahneman describes two systems we use for thinking and solving problems.[65] System 1 is the *fast* mode. It works automatically and unconsciously. System 1 is the realm of immediate judgment; we know instantly, for example, that two plus two equals four, and we can usually discern with reasonable accuracy the mood of a friend by the tone of her voice on the telephone.

System 2 is the *slow* mode. It is rational and deliberate. System 2 is the realm of careful analysis. You use it when you edit something you've written or when you try to solve a more complicated math problem.

System 1 looks at a suspect's gangsta demeanor and hears that he has a criminal record, and immediately decides "Guilty!" System 2 considers all the evidence and renders a deliberate and more careful verdict. (That's why a jury is asked to deliberate.)

Consider this simple problem adapted from Kahneman's book: A pen and a pencil cost $1.10. The pen costs one dollar more than the pencil. How much does the pencil cost? Almost everyone responds, "Ten cents." That's the System 1 response. It's fast, effortless, and feels intuitively right. But it's wrong.

You must engage System 2 to calculate. The correct answer is five cents. The pen cost $1.05 and the pencil $.05, totaling $1.10. If the answer were $.10, then the total cost would be $1.20.

This problem highlights an intriguing question raised by Kahneman's work—a question that is at the heart of understanding the creative process and our quest for creative lives: *how do we know when to trust our intuitions and when to challenge them?*

Without System 1, we wouldn't be able to function effectively in our daily lives. If we had to do deliberate thinking to tie our shoes and brush our teeth, we would never get out of the house. But System 1 also leads us astray. It's responsible for our susceptibility to manipulation by advertisers and marketers (for example, shoppers buy more of a product when they are told that "supplies are limited"). And it regularly leads people to make unwise investment decisions because those decisions require disciplined analysis. As Kahneman explains, "People are not accustomed to thinking hard and are often content to trust a plausible judgment that comes quickly to mind."[66]

Kahneman emphasizes that System 2 is often reluctant to engage, and it takes effort to use it. Playwright and critic George Bernard Shaw (1856–1950) captured the challenge of deploying System 2 when he quipped, "People hate thinking. They will do almost anything to avoid it. I have made an international reputation for myself by doing it once or twice a week."[67]

The biggest misconception associated with creativity (besides the notion that it can't be learned) is that it's all about intuition and "thinking out of the box," and that logical deliberation isn't necessary. Just as deliberate practice is necessary to improve in any skill, deliberate thinking is required to find and implement creative ideas. The key is to know when to access each mode of thinking and how to move fluidly between them. If we are locked into a deliberate mode, then we are too slow and unwieldy. If we just go by hunches and first impressions, we are apt to be prejudiced and to make costly errors.

Creativity requires a dialogue between systems 1 and 2. We must learn to find a balance between our intuitive abilities and deliberate reasoning.

Mind Mapping's nonlinear format means that you can start anywhere and go in any direction at any time. This, combined with the use of color and images, makes it easier to get access to the savvier aspects of your fast thinking. And by displaying information clearly in a big picture with printed key words, Mind Mapping encourages the careful reflection and disciplined, deliberate analysis that characterize System 2.

System 3: Thinking Outside of Time

Kahneman's work with System 1 and System 2 thinking is brilliant, and being able to shift between the two is vital to mastering the creative process. But he's missing something—a third mode of thinking that I call System 3.

System 1 is everyday intuition. System 2 is deliberate thinking. System 3 is higher intuition. System 1 is fast. System 2 is slow. System 3 is outside of time.

For forty years, I've been exploring how to access System 3 thinking and have experienced many powerful methods for awakening deeper creativity. All of these methods have one element in common: they help us to shift out of our habitual perceptions. There's a thin veil that separates our quotidian lives from our creative source. The challenge is to shift out of habitual perception, open to the creative source, and then integrate what was learned in the shift, without dissociating. Understanding the five phases of the creative process helps us to contextualize and ground our leaps into the unknown.

Many people have profound creative insights, for example, under the influence of mind-altering drugs, but they sometimes alter their neural chemistry in ways that can interfere with healthy functioning. It may be possible, with expert guidance, to use pharmaceuticals in a constructive manner, but there are safer approaches to get the same results. Drumming, chanting, dancing, yoga, fasting, deep contemplation, and meditation are just some of the ways that people in cultures throughout the world have increased their receptivity to creative insight.

The craziness that is often associated with very imaginative individuals is a function of their inability to ground and integrate the deeper perceptions and powerful insights that come when, as William Blake phrased it, "the doors of perception" are cleansed.[68]

How can you transcend your mundane awareness in a way that is relatively easy to integrate? Just pick up a pen and "go write to the source."

Go Write to the Source

> Fill your paper with the breathings of your heart.
> William Wordsworth[69]

What do Leonardo da Vinci, Thomas Edison, Charles Darwin, Marie Curie, and many other great creative minds all have in common? They all kept notebooks or journals. And their notebooks were often disorganized and filled with creative doodling.

When Leonardo, for example, woke up at three o'clock in the morning with a wacky, off-the-wall idea, he wrote it down in his notebook. When the average person wakes up at three o'clock in the morning with a wacky, off-the-wall idea, he usually rolls over and goes back to sleep. Poet

Mary Oliver explains, "It's very important to write things down instantly . . . I have a rule that if I wake up at three in the morning and think of something, I write it down. I can't wait until morning—it'll be gone."[70]

Recording and exploring your ideas in writing is one of the simplest ways to access deeper creative insight. Philosopher John Locke (1632–1704) advised, "The thoughts that often come unsought, and, as it were, drop into the mind, are commonly the most valuable of any we have, and therefore should be secured, because they seldom return again."[71]

The challenge for most people, however, is based on the kind of writing they did at school and the writing they must do as professionals. If you're a student, then your essays must have a clear beginning, middle, and end, with a logical thematic progression; if they don't, you get a poor grade. If you must write for your job, then your reports or proposals, for example, must follow a clear linear progression, and there are often serious negative consequences for inaccuracies and mistakes.

The writing we do in school and in the office doesn't encourage our connection to deeper creativity. If you want access to System 3, to the universal field of creativity, the simplest method is to write in a nonlinear, free-flowing fashion without any regard whatsoever for what others may think.

There are many methods for doing this, including those taught by Julia Cameron (morning pages), Natalie Goldberg (*Writing Down the Bones*), Mark Levy (freewriting), Linda Trichter Metcalf (Proprioceptive Writing), and others. All of these methods facilitate greater access to System 3. What they have in common is the practice of not censoring your expression and writing against some kind of limit, either time (ten to twenty-five minutes) or length (three 8 1/2 x 11" pages). And they all require you to write longhand, not on the computer.

The key variables between the approaches are the time of day and the extent to which you read and reflect on what you've written. Julia Cameron's morning pages are done first thing in the morning. When you first arise, your mind is closer to what psychologists call a hypnopompic state, a brainwave state associated with creative insight. Cameron asks that you do not read or reflect on what you've written as you write it, whereas Metcalf recommends that when meaningful, intriguing, or highly charged words emerge in your writing, you reflect upon them through what she calls the proprioceptive question ("What do I mean by ____?"). Although proprioception usually refers to our kinesthetic sense, Metcalf uses it to refer to the mind's ability to communicate with itself. As she explains, "The body knows itself through its proprioceptive sense, and through this kind of writing the mind comes to know itself."[72] Metcalf also recommends that you light a candle and play baroque music as you write. The candle and music ease your brainwaves into a state that is similar to the mode you are in when you arise.

All of these methods yield powerful results. So read the book and take the course of the one that appeals to you the most. (See "Recommended Resources.")

In the meantime, you can experiment with the "Go Write to the Source" protocol that I've developed to help you get the experience of accessing System 3 with the least amount of time and effort. This isn't primarily a writing exercise as much as a means to free yourself from habitual constraints and access a deeper creative voice. But if you've always wanted to write something—a screenplay, novel, nonfiction book, or memoir—then you'll discover that it can be a wonderful way to get started. Either way, just do it! As professional writers know, if you wait to write, you're not a writer; you're a waiter.

Preparing to Go Write to the Source

Begin by invoking the Muse in whatever terms are most natural for you. It's best to write out a request in your notebook and/or say it aloud. In your own words, affirm something like, "I ask for the guidance of (God, the Holy Spirit, the Muses, my intuition, the core of the universe, System 3) to gain insight into (your creative challenge) for the highest good."

Then in one session, write out one hundred questions in stream-of-consciousness style. Start writing questions and don't lift your pen off the paper until you've completed a hundred. The questions can focus on anything that arises, from "What's my deepest purpose?" to "How deep are porpoises?" Don't worry about spelling, grammar, or neatness.

Just keep writing questions. Many people discover that the first twenty or thirty questions aren't necessarily the most inspired, but in the next twenty or thirty, themes begin to arise. And in the last part of the exercise it's not unusual for profound material to emerge.

When you've completed your list, read it through and circle the ten questions that inspire you the most. Then copy these ten power questions on a separate piece of paper.

Of all the exercises in *How to Think Like Leonardo da Vinci,* this one generated the most positive response from readers. Brian Johnson, creator of PhilosophersNotes and founder and CEO of en*theos, explains the effect this exercise had on his creative process: "I did the 100 Questions exercise on June 8, 2001. Much to my surprise and amazement, I was propelled way beyond my ordinary thinking. I experienced a direct connection to a deeper source of creative inspiration. The 10 'power questions' I identified have been guiding my life ever since."[73]

Do the hundred questions exercise to initiate your "Go Write to the Source" exploration. The exercise stimulates your curiosity and inspires a renaissance of your creative birthright.

How to Practice the Go Write to the Source Protocol

You can do the protocol focusing on an important creative challenge in your life. Perhaps you are still working on clarifying your purpose and trying to figure out how to get paid for doing what you love. Maybe you want to retire or change careers and are aiming to discover what to do next. Whether you are generating ideas for a new screenplay or novel, or planning a business venture or focusing on a relationship issue, you can use this exercise to shift out of your habitual modalities and into a connection with a deeper source. You can also benefit without a specific theme or problem focus; your System 3 wisdom will come through nonetheless.

If possible, set aside the same time each day for this exercise. There can be, as Julia Cameron counsels, a special benefit to doing it first thing in the morning, but that doesn't work for everyone. Some people find that doing the exercise before going to sleep at night helps to inspire their incubatory facility. Find the time that works best for you and stick to it for three weeks.

Begin by doing the qi-cultivation practice that feels best for you. Most people find that they are much more creative in this exercise when they begin with ten minutes of the Simple Standing Meditation, Cloud Hands Practice, or Shifting Modes Practice, for example.

After your qi cultivation, you will do ten minutes of free-flow writing. For the first five minutes of each writing session, write continuously, as fast as you can without straining. Keep your pen moving even if it seems that you are writing gibberish. Then after those five minutes, feel free to continue writing fast, or slow down and reflect on words and phrases that are meaningful in the moment.

You can attune your brainwaves to be more receptive to creative insight by playing music as you write. Baroque, jazz, Indian raga, or Gregorian chants are particularly helpful. Candles or incense are optional.

If you need a prompt to help you start your writing, reread your list of one hundred questions, choose one, and respond to it. Do not, however, feel constrained to stay on that theme. Let your associations flow freely, without editing.

If you get stuck or feel uncomfortable or bored at any time during the exercise, then write about what it feels like to be uncomfortable and bored. And/or switch hands and continue writing with your nondominant hand. And/or do another qi-cultivation practice.

Go with the flow. Avoid editing. This is a Generation Phase method, so go for quantity, suspend the expression of judgment, and have fun and seek the unfamiliar.

After each period of seven days, read everything you have written that week.

Have your notebook with you throughout the day and keep it by your bed at night when you are undertaking this exploration. This exercise will stimulate your connection to System 3, and you will discover that you are getting more ideas in the shower, car, or bed. Be sure to record those ideas in your notebook, especially if they seem wacky or off-the-wall.

Twenty minutes a day for three weeks is enough for almost everyone to experience the benefits. And once you experience the benefits, you will probably want to continue.

Q and A   Mastering the Creative Process

Q *How much time do I spend in each phase of the creative process?*

A There are no rules for the amount of time you spend in each phase. The time you devote will be a function of the total time available. Keep in mind that just as it's best to sharpen a saw before cutting wood, it's good to ensure that you invest sufficient time in the Preparation Phase.

As you bring more attention to the flow of the creative process, you'll develop your blue-hat ability to shift into the right mode at the right time.

Q *How do I apply the creative process with a group?*

A Begin by introducing everyone to the elements of the creative mindset and the concept of different phases, hats, and intelligences. The awareness and acceptance of the idea of different modes of thinking will elevate all of your discourse.

The process of developing and implementing creative ideas can be compared to gardening. Ideas often start as delicate, little seedlings that need to be carefully nurtured on an individual basis. Then they can be put into bigger pots to strengthen their roots in the greenhouse—the equivalent of small groups—and then they're ready to live in the real garden.

So, for example, in the Preparation Phase, begin by asking each individual to generate her own thoughts on the nature of the creative challenge, independently. Then move into small groups (four is the optimal number, but three or five is also fine) and share the ideas. The most effective way to do this sharing is to allot a set amount of time for each member of the group to speak while everyone else listens empathically. It's best to proceed in reverse order of seniority, so that junior people don't feel intimidated or influenced by the ideas of more senior folks. This greenhouse approach to ideas facilitates inclusion and prevents the domination of the process by the most extroverted, expressive, or authoritative person in the group.

Give everyone a chance, over time, to play the role of facilitator. As different people play this role, your group matures in its understanding of the creative process. And, whenever possible, share qi-cultivation practices together. You'll discover greater freedom to shift modes appropriately, more energy for the tasks at hand, and enhanced esprit de corps.

Q *What's the role of debate and argument in the creative process?*

A Debate, argument, and lively discussion are very important elements of the creative process. The secret is to avoid getting into this mode prematurely, before everyone has had a chance to think things through and express their ideas. After you've presented the cases from both the angel's advocate and the devil's advocate, open the discussion and encourage debate. As teams mature and gain experience in applying the creative process, they become less politically correct, more authentic, and better at arguing intelligently.

Q *What are the biggest problems in most approaches to solving problems?*

A **Trying to find solutions before reviewing the data and defining the real problem.** In other words, omitting or abbreviating the Preparation Phase

Rushing into evaluation. Short-circuiting the generation mode through impatience and intolerance for seemingly crazy ideas.

Insufficient time devoted to incubation. Many groups get together for just one day—or worse, just a morning or afternoon—in an attempt to solve a significant problem. This does not leave enough time for incubation. Whenever possible, creative problem-solving, planning, or strategy sessions should take place over the course of at least two days. The creativity and productivity of these sessions go up dramatically when you allow time to literally sleep on it. If you've ever had the experience of agreeing to terms in a negotiation and then, perhaps while driving home, suddenly thinking of something that you neglected to include, then you realize the importance of building in time for incubation in all of your thinking and decision-making.

Wearing a yellow or black hat with a hidden red lining. Many people unconsciously support or oppose an idea because of vested interest, ego, or prejudice. Lack of self-awareness, more than willful obnoxiousness, remains the greatest obstacle to effective creativity in both individuals and groups.

Failing to decide and neglecting to plan for implementation. Many "creative" efforts end before anything is accomplished. People get together, dump lots of ideas on flip charts, hang them on the wall, and go home. They may have generated many potentially valuable ideas and had some good laughs, but without a focus on evaluation and implementation, nothing is created.

Running out of energy. Qi fuels the creative process. Individuals and groups who don't know how to cultivate it will often experience a sense of depletion and disenchantment, especially when solutions are elusive and ambiguity is high.

Q *I've read research stating that brainstorming doesn't work. Why do you recommend it?*

A The research that supposedly demonstrates that brainstorming doesn't work was highlighted in a *New Yorker* article citing Keith Sawyer, a psychologist from Washington University, as follows: "Decades of research have consistently shown that brainstorming groups think of far fewer ideas than the same number of people who work alone and later pool their ideas."[74]

Brainstorming that is done improperly is ineffective. If you begin in a group and ask people to share ideas without criticizing them, you will not get much of a response. Brainstorming should begin with individuals working alone first and then pooling their ideas in the greenhouse manner described previously.

The article also cites the research of Charlan Nemeth, a psychologist at UC Berkeley, demonstrating that groups who engage in vigorous debate generate more ideas than those who are given no instructions or those who are asked to generate ideas without criticizing them. But Nemeth's experiment failed to include a group that was asked to first generate ideas without criticizing and then debate them, which is what I recommend that you do.

Q *You suggest that we ask, "What problems may be caused by solving this problem?" Could you please explain and give an example?*

A On the global political level, the United States aimed to solve the problem of the attempt at world domination by the former Soviet Union. In Afghanistan, the Americans trained and armed the Mujahideen, who successfully drove out the Soviets. But they failed to anticipate that the Mujahideen would become the Taliban. (If you saw the movie *Charlie Wilson's War*, then you know the details.) In Iran, the United States helped depose Mohammad Mosaddegh (1882–1967), the democratically elected left-wing ruler, and installed the shah, thereby giving rise to the ayatollahs.

In healthcare, a significant percentage of illnesses are iatrogenic. In other words, they are caused by the treatment. Antibiotics may solve the problem of a current infection but also may be the cause of a future infection.

The solution to every problem has the potential to create new problems, so it's useful to think ahead in a systems-oriented, holistic fashion.

Q *Does creativity emerge from a divine source?*

There is no difference between the Creator and creation,
just as there is no difference between the ocean and its waves.

Amma, Indian saint[75]

A   Throughout history geniuses have expressed their connection to a divine creator.

William Blake writes, "I myself do nothing. The Holy Spirit accomplishes all through me."[76]

Johannes Brahms credits the source of his creativity: "Straightaway the ideas flow in upon me, directly from God."[77]

Music legend Johnny Cash (1932–2003) explains, "Creative people have to be fed from the divine source."[78]

Visionary inventor Nikola Tesla observed, "The gift of mental power comes from God, Divine Being, and if we concentrate our minds on that truth, we become in tune with this great power."[79] He adds, "We have, undoubtedly, certain finer fibers that enable us to perceive truths when logical deduction, or any other willful effort of the brain, is futile."[80]

Holy Spirit, God, and *Divine Being* are different expressions of the experience of System 3. This is the state where the "finer fibers" that Tesla mentioned attune to the creative broadcast. It is the key to accessing higher creativity and the portal for profound inspiration. You don't have to believe in a particular religion or spiritual path in order to access this state.

Q   *Can you summarize the benefits of qi cultivation for the creative process?*

A   The question that is at the heart of understanding the creative process and our quest for creative lives is, how do we know when to trust our intuition and when to challenge it? The greatest benefit of these practices is that they enhance your kinesthetic-energetic awareness so you can get more in touch with the messages of your guts, blood, bones, and heart—the whispers of your intuitive wisdom. As you practice, you will tune the antenna so you get better reception, and you will be better able to hear your own true voice. Regular qi cultivation will also give you the verve and stamina you need to build the foundation for the castles your imagination constructs.

PART 4

MASTERING CREATIVE ENERGY, MINDSET, and PROCESS:
Moving from Force to Power

To become more conscious is the greatest gift
anyone can give to the world; moreover, in a ripple effect
the gift comes back to its source.

David R. Hawkins, MD, PhD (1927–2012), author of Power vs. Force[1]

When I was growing up in New Jersey, it gradually became apparent that limited consciousness was the reason for the dearth of creativity and compassion in the world. Our local newspaper, *The Herald News,* expressed the level of consciousness in the state with an unforgettable headline reporting on the score of a basketball game between two Catholic schools: "Immaculate Conception Blows Out Queen of Peace!"

In *Power vs. Force,* physician David R. Hawkins presents a compelling guide for anyone interested in exploring his or her state of consciousness and creative energy, mindset, and process. Hawkins presents a scale, from 20 to 1,000, showing an evolution from lesser states of consciousness (the realm he refers to as Force) to more enlightened states (the realm he refers to as Power). The realm of Force, to which Hawkins assigns a value on his scale of 199 or lower, is the province of shame, guilt, apathy, dependency, fear, desire (craving), anger, and pride. As Hawkins explains, we can awaken our consciousness by simply becoming aware of the different levels. Awareness promotes empathy, empathy supports compassion, and compassion is higher on the scale.

The realm of Power includes the following levels (with the quantitative measure assigned by Hawkins and a brief explanation):

1. Courage (200). Here we embrace the challenges of life and commit to growth. Courage is the beginning of a creative mindset. Rollo May explains, "Courage is not a virtue of value among other personal values like love or fidelity. It is the foundation that underlies and gives reality to all other virtues and personal values. Without courage our love pales into mere dependency. Without courage our fidelity becomes conformism."[2]

2. Neutrality (250). The beginning of the capacity for nonjudgmental awareness.

3. Willingness (310). At this level, the creative mindset is now well established. Every experience is embraced as an opportunity for growth and learning. Willingness also looks for ways to contribute to others.

4. Acceptance (350). This is the level at which an individual accepts full responsibility for her life and what she creates.

5. Reason (400). Here we discover the clear, advanced, deliberate thinking that allows us to be truly creative.

6. Love (500). At this level, we experience forgiveness, compassion, and unconditional love.

7. Joy (540). This is the level at which we experience the perfection of creation and the true beauty of life. As William Wordsworth expressed it, "With an eye made quiet by the power of harmony, and the deep power of joy, we see into the life of things."[3]

8. Peace (600). Here we experience our oneness with all creation. This is "the peace that passes all understanding."

9. Enlightenment (700–1000). The level of the great teachers of humanity. It is timeless, nondual, abiding in permanent grace. Now you realize that the idea of levels of consciousness is an illusion. You are one with the source of consciousness and creativity.

Qi Cultivation for Moving from Force to Power[4]

This practice offers a guided tour of the nine levels of consciousness. It can help you raise your baseline of creative energy as it supports a more creative mindset and tunes your antenna to be more receptive to System 3. As Hawkins explains, genius is "a style of consciousness characterized by the ability to access high-energy attractor patterns."[5] This practice will align you with those high-energy attractor patterns.

Force-to-Power Practice

In this practice, you will go through movements or postures that represent and embody each level of consciousness. As you take this guided tour of your own potential, you can use each step as a means to attune to the energy at that level. I recommend that the first few times you do this practice you do all the movements in a single session and in the sequence presented.

Preparation: Releasing Force, Embracing Power

Begin in the basic standing posture. Close your eyes and smile. Sink your energy through the Bubbling Spring points deep into the earth, even as your apex points up to the sky. Keeping your feet in full contact with the ground, begin bouncing by rhythmically bending and unbending your knees. Allow your arms to flop around freely. Let your head move like a buoy bobbing gently on the surface of water.

Gradually increase the vigor of the bouncing and shaking with childlike glee and abandon. Continue for two minutes, and as you do imagine shaking yourself free from Force-related habits.

As you continue to bounce, breathe naturally and visualize a golden wave of light traveling down from the sky, flooding your upper center with golden light. Then draw that light down through your chest and arms, down to your waist, and through your legs. Sink the light through your Bubbling Spring points down deep into the earth. Imagine that the light is purifying your Force-related tendencies. Repeat this visualization as often as you like as you continue to bounce for two minutes.

After two minutes, stop bouncing and feel the enlivened energy throughout your system. Then inhale as you raise both arms up over your head and shake them three times. As you exhale, make an extended *haaahh* sound and release your arms down toward the ground, letting go of any remaining attachment to Force. Repeat three times.

Then extend your arms and allow them to rise up so that your hands are stretching up to the sky above your head, palms facing each other, like a football referee signaling a touchdown. Relax your hands so the palms face toward the top of your head, and gently lower your hands in front of your body, drawing heavenly qi through your upper, middle, and lower centers. Allow the qi to wash away any remnants of your Force-related tendencies. Repeat three to seven times.

Movement 1. Courage: The Creative Warrior Draws the Bow

Begin with your hands in prayer position in front of your middle center. Take a wide stance, feet about twice shoulder width apart (find the distance that is comfortable for you).

With a lengthening spine, sink your body by bending your knees and extend your left arm out to the left side. Your right hand forms a soft fist and pulls back to the right shoulder nest as though you were drawing a bowstring. The tip of the left index finger moves toward your left thumb, without touching it, to form a C shape. Gaze through the gap between your index and middle fingers.

Allow your heart to open, and enjoy the dynamic tension between your extended left hand and the elbow of your right arm, which is stretching in the opposite direction.

To shift to the other side, begin with a blink of your eyes. Then sweep your left hand back to the center of your body. Allow your right hand to intersect with the left to form a V shape, with your right hand on the inside. Then extend your right hand out to the right side and pull your left fist back to the left shoulder nest. Look through the space between your right index and middle fingers, and remember to keep your heart open. (See figure 2.3.)

Repeat the pose seven times on each side. Finish by nourishing your qi.

Movement 2. Neutrality: Standing in the Field of Creative Potential

Adopt the basic standing posture. As you exhale, let your body sink down slightly as your arms float up to create a diamond shape in front of you, with your fingertips (maintain space between the fingers) at the level of your navel. (See figure 3.3.) This is an ancient posture of neutrality. Rest in this posture for three to seven breaths. Put your attention on the negative space around you.

Movement 3. Willingness: Exploring New Horizons

From the basic standing posture, widen your stance and turn your toes out a bit so that your knees will stay in alignment with your feet as you move.

Slip your left hand behind your back and support your right kidney with the back of your left hand. Now scoop your right hand, palm facing up, out to the left, across the horizon in front of you, toward your left side (figure 4.1). Sweep the right hand back across the horizon in front of your body.

When your right hand reaches the right side of the horizon, bring it around behind your torso and lay the back of it against your left kidney to support it. At the same time, move your left hand away from your back and sweep it, palm up, out to the right and across the horizon in front of you.

Avoid stretching either arm too far beyond the boundaries of your feet. As you move, bend your knees and shift your weight in an integrated and comfortable fashion. Be sure

figure 4.1 The Force-to-Power Practice, Movement 3

that you are breathing easily. Once you discover a comfortable way to make these movements, you can allow your eyes to follow each hand as it sweeps across the horizon.

Repeat the movement of each arm seven times. After the last repetition, bring both hands behind the back, with the back of the right hand supporting the right kidney and the back of the left hand supporting the left kidney.

Movement 4. Acceptance: Blending with the Universe

From your position at the end of movement 3, gently arch your back and massage your kidneys with the backs of your hands as you draw your hands forward, around and in front of your body. Let your arms and hands settle, palms up, forearms parallel to the ground, elbows resting close to either side of the torso. (See figure 4.2.) Pause and enjoy this position of acceptance.

Then gently sweep both arms up in half-moon arcs. Your palms face in toward one another and up to the sky, at about the height

figure 4.2 The Force-to-Power Practice, Movement 4, first position

of your head top. Avoid raising your shoulders. (See figure 4.3.) Keeping your arms raised, inhale and allow your gaze to go up toward the sky, then exhale and look down to the ground in front of you. Breathe and move your gaze from sky to earth three more times. Then bring your hands down and let your palms rest on your lower center.

figure 4.3 The Force-to-Power Practice, Movement 4, second position

Movement 5. Reason: Piercing the Heavens

Shift your weight to your left foot and place your left hand in front of your lower center, palm facing down. Concentrate your energy on the outside of your left arm, as though you were blocking a kick. Your right hand sweeps up the midline of your torso, with an open, taut palm (the same movement as an uppercut in boxing, but with an open hand instead of a fist). Your right hand energetically pierces through prejudice and irrationality, and opens the realm of reason. Then shift to the right side as the right hand blocks and the left hand pierces upward. Repeat each side seven times. When finished, place both palms on your lower center again.

Movement 6. Love: Embracing All Creation

From the basic standing posture, shift your weight onto your right foot. Bring your hands and arms up and cross them at chest level, as though you were hugging someone you love with all your heart (as if you were cradling that person's head and upper body; see figure 4.4). Then shift your weight to the left foot and gently switch your hands and arms, again cradling your loved one's head and upper body. Gently rock back and forth between these positions; as you do, feel the energy of pure love and compassion for all creation, including yourself. Repeat each side eight times. Finish by standing still, dropping your arms, and returning your palms to your lower center.

figure 4.4   The Force-to-Power Practice, Movement 6

Movement 7. Joy: The Distillation of Wonder

Begin in the basic standing posture. Bring all the fingertips of your left hand together and point them upwards, with the pinky-finger side of your left wrist resting near your lower belly. Bring the fingertips of the right hand together, and with the right-thumb side of your right hand facing your body, touch the fingertips of the right hand against the fingertips of your left hand. (See figure 4.5.) Rotate your left wrist in a clockwise direction and your right wrist counterclockwise to create a helix-like movement (figure 4.6). As you rotate your wrists, both elbows move away from your body. Then allow the fingers to unwind and return to their original meeting place, as the elbows move back toward your body.

Leave the left hand where it is and draw your right wrist, fingers still facing downward, delicately up to the level of the point of perception. This movement is sometimes called "silk reeling," and the feeling, as you draw the right hand up, is as though you were reeling out a gossamer strand of energetic silk. As your right hand reaches the point of perception, gently open the fingers of both hands. Allow the hands to describe the circumference of a sphere, with the right hand flowing down and the left hand floating up.

When the left hand is in front of the point of perception, palm downward, and the right hand is in front of the lower center, palm up, enjoy

figure 4.5 The Force-to-Power Practice, Movement 7, first hand position

a generous inhalation and stretch the left hand up toward the sky, as though you were energetic pulling taffy vertically. As you bring your left hand back downward, bring the fingertips of each hand together again, so they meet at the level of your lower center.

Now the left wrist rotates in a clockwise direction and the right counterclockwise. As you screw the fingertips together, imagine that you are concentrating the essence of joy in the core of your being. As your wrists and fingertips unscrew and your left hand floats up your center line, the right hand remains at the lower center, fingertips pointing up. As the left hand reaches the point of perception, gently open the fingers of both hands, caressing the circumference of the energy sphere, with the left hand rotating down and the right hand rotating up.

When the right hand reaches the front of the point of perception, palm downward, and the left hand is in front of the lower center, palm up, enjoy a generous inhalation and stretch the right hand up toward the sky, as though you were energetic pulling taffy vertically.

figure 4.6 From the first hand position, rotate the wrists in opposite directions. Then lift the right hand up to the point of perception.

Repeat the entire movement seven times. Finish with the palms facing one another, with one hand at the point of perception and the other at the lower center.

figure 4.7 The Force-to-Power Practice, Movement 8

Movement 8. Peace: The Sphere of Serenity

From the position at the end of movement 7, slowly rotate your separated hands around the circumference of the sphere of energy in front of your body (figure 4.7). As you caress the sphere, you experience joy becoming deep peace. After seven rotations around the sphere, begin to slowly compress the size of the sphere by making gradually smaller movements with your hands until you are describing a concentrated sphere, about the size of a tennis ball, in front of your lower center (figure 4.8). Bring your palms together on top of your lower center. As you do, place the sphere inside your lower center.

Movement 9. Enlightenment: Universal Posture

With your eyes closed, place your right hand an inch or so in front of your chest. The hand should be vertical, with your fingers pointing up toward the sky. Your right palm is open toward your left side; your thumb is toward your sternum. Place your left hand just underneath your navel, with your palm facing up. (See figure 1.6.)

Breathe slowly and deeply, bow your head slightly, and surrender your entire being to the creative power of the universe. Stand in this universal posture for one minute.

Complete the Force-to-Power Practice by returning to the starting posture and nourishing your qi.

figure 4.8 Slowly compress your energy sphere until it is the size of a tennis ball.

WHO MOVED MY QI?

In 1982, I moved to Washington, DC, the place where I believed that creativity was most urgently needed. I was disappointed to discover that most politicians had no interest in creativity or innovation. Although I didn't get the chance to influence our political leaders, I did meet and work with some interesting people, including members of a US Army think tank who were working on a new idea they called "the net"—a system to allow people around the world to share knowledge and communicate instantly via computer. In 1985, I led a five-day residential seminar on creativity for a group of eighty army officers and worked with members of the legendary First Earth Battalion, featured many years later in the book and movie *The Men Who Stare at Goats.*

"The net" that my army clients were developing became one of the major technological developments of our time, and along with smartphones, it has contributed to the pressure for everything to be instant, "on demand."

The demand for speed has driven the development of what seems to be the next great technological shift: *the Internet of Things.* The term was coined in 1999 by the English technology innovator Kevin Ashton, who explains, "If we had computers that knew everything there was to know about things—using data they gathered without any help from us—we would be able to track and count everything, and greatly reduce waste, loss and cost. We would know when things needed replacing, repairing or recalling, and whether they were fresh or past their best. The Internet of Things has the potential to change the world, just as the

Internet did. Maybe even more so."[1] In January 2014 I was invited to give a keynote address on creativity to a conference of senior executives from many of the world's most powerful companies who were seeking to utilize the Internet of Things to radically increase the productivity and effectiveness of their global operations.

The theme of the first corporate seminar I led in 1979 was "utilizing creativity to deal with accelerating change." That theme continues to be extremely popular today. In the introduction to this book, I noted that none of us on that 1979 program, including myself, predicted the extraordinary changes of the last thirty-five years. It's reasonable to assume that developments in technology, communication, business, and society over the next thirty-five years will also be surprising.

As the world changes in ways that we may not be able to anticipate, it becomes more important to focus on unchanging values and universal truths. One of the mottos I've created to help us remember this is *Aut veritas universale aut totum stercora* ("It's either universal truth or it is bullshit").

One of the most important universal truths, implicit throughout this book, is that *to speed up effectively you must learn to slow down.* If, for example, you want to be able to use tai chi as a martial art, to move with lightning speed, you must first practice the form slowly, so that the movements are made precisely and integrated into your neuromuscular system. The secret to accelerating your progress, doing more with less, and working constructively is to slow down internally and manage your energy, rather than being seduced by the illusion that you can manage time.

Creativity On Demand draws on timeless wisdom to help us meet the challenges of our crazy times. The infinite field of creative energy is there for us on demand. If you invest a little time to practice every day, you'll discover that you can tune into this field whenever you want and use it to fulfill your creative dreams and meet the demands of everyday life in more creative ways.

In the late 1970s I attended the lectures held at Brockwood Park in England by author and sage J. Krishnamurti (1895–1986). When he took the stage, his first words were, "There is no speaker." I believe that he meant that everything we perceive is our own projection, and we must be responsible and not depend on "the speaker" to enlighten us. (At the lunch break, I was in the queue for food, and Krishnamurti himself happened to get in line behind me. I was tempted to say, "There is no lunch line," but managed to restrain myself.)

Krishnamurti's line of reasoning from a talk he gave in Delhi in 1965 is relevant to all seekers of creative consciousness: "It seems to me that the real problem is the mind itself, and not the problem which the mind has created and tries to solve. If the mind is petty, small, narrow, limited, however great and complex the problem may be, the mind approaches that problem in terms of its own pettiness. If I have a little mind and I think of God, the God of my thinking will be a little God."[2]

He asks, "Can the mind that is small, petty, be transformed into something which is not bound by its own limitations?"[3] And elsewhere he hints at the answer: "It is only that energy which is not the product of thought that is creative."[4] A creative mindset and an understanding of the creative process can help us move beyond a mind that is small, petty, and fixed, but the missing link, as Krishnamurti suggests, is the energy.

Spencer Johnson, author of *Who Moved My Cheese?*, reminds us that the world won't stop changing and we must adapt our expectations and become more comfortable with uncertainty. Deepak Malhotra, author of *I Moved Your Cheese,* emphasizes the importance of a creative mindset in managing change. Now my wish for you is that you'll discover that the essential issue isn't who moves your cheese, but rather how you move your qi.

Acknowledgments

I'm grateful to the masters of energy arts who contributed their insight, expertise, and qi directly to this book: Ken Cohen, the Barefoot Doctor (aka Stephen Russell), Dean Y. Deng, Alan Finger, Mingtong Gu, Al Huang, Roger Jahnke, Wendy Palmer, Robert Peng, Robert Tangora, and Michael Winn.

Ahéhee' to the teachers who influenced the creation of this book: J. G. Bennett, Mort Herskowitz, Harvey Konigsberg, Shuren Ma, Clyde Takeguchi, and The Anonymous Master. And to all the teachers of all of my teachers.

Grazie mille to my friends who read the manuscript at various stages and shared constructive criticism: Barbara Bonfigli, Margot Borden, Leslie (The Duck) Copland, Caryn Cridland, Lorie Dechar, Brian Johnson, Donna Pace, Dale Schusterman, Stasia Siena, and Jason Voss. Special thanks to Felicity Broennan.

Xiè xie ni to the "Creators on Qi": Jim Alexander, Jane Barthelemy, Carol Rose Brown, Kaleo and Elise Ching, Lorie Dechar, Bill Douglas, Bill Gallen, Jon Miller, and Vanda North.

Merci beaucoup to: Frank Allen, Steve Bhaerman, Tony Buzan, Julia Cameron, John Cleese, Edward de Bono, Carol Dweck, Amy Elizabeth Fox, Murray Gell-Mann, Ira Glass, Forrest Hainline, Raymond Keene, Fred Milder, Jim Mungle, Karen Page, Steven Pressfield, Raj Sisodia, Burt Swersey, John Voigt, and Tina Zhang. And to all my practice partners at Tangora Tai Chi and The MogaDao Institute.

Big thanks to the wonderful folks from Sounds True: Jennifer Brown, Chris Covey, Jennifer Holder, Jennifer Miles, and Tami Simon.

Extra special thanks to:

Robert Peng for translating an ancient lineage into contemporary terms with grace, power, and joy.

Robert Tangora for enriching my understanding of the practical power of qi.

Ken Robinson for his wonderful foreword.

Amy Rost for incisive, brilliant editing.

My parents, Joan and Sandy Gelb, for their inspiration and love.

My wife, Deborah Domanski, for her exquisite embodiment and expression of the creative power of the universe.

LIST *of* QI-CULTIVATION PRACTICES

201

Recommended Resources

Alexander Technique (alexandertechniqueworkshops.com)

Frank Allen and Tina Zhang, Wu Tang Physical Culture Association (wutangpca.com)

Jane Barthelemy, Jane's Healthy Kitchen (janeshealthykitchen.com)

Steve Bhaerman (Swami Beyondananda), Wake Up Laughing (wakeuplaughing.com)

Margot Borden, Integral Perspectives (margotborden.com)

Carol Rose Brown (carolrosebrown.com)

Tony Buzan (tonybuzan.com)

Sarah Miller Caldicott (powerpatterns.com)

Julia Cameron, Julia Cameron Live/The Artist's Way (juliacameronlive.com)

Kaleo Ching and Elise Dirlam Ching (kaleoching.com)

James G. S. Clawson (faculty.darden.virginia.edu/clawsonj)

Ken Cohen, Healing Ways: The Teachings of Kenneth Cohen (qigonghealing.com)

Edward de Bono (edwdebono.com)

Lorie Dechar, Five Spirits (fivespirits.com)

Dean Y. Deng, MD, Acucenter Pain Clinic (acucenter-pain-clinic.com)

Deborah Domanski (deborahdomanski.com)

Bill Douglas, Stress Management and Relaxation Technology Productions (SMARTaichi.com)

Carol Dweck, Mindset (mindsetonline.com)

Alan Finger, ISHTA Yoga (ishtayoga.com)

Amy Elizabeth Fox, Mobius Executive Leadership (mobiusleadership.com)

Robert Fritz, Robert Fritz, Inc. (robertfritz.com)

Bill Gallen (billgallen.com)

Natalie Goldberg (nataliegoldberg.com)

Mingtong Gu, The Chi Center (chicenter.com)

Chungliang Al Huang, Living Tao Foundation (livingtao.org)

Roger Jahnke, OMD, Institute of Integral Qigong and Tai Chi (iiqtc.org)

Michelle James, The Center for Creative Emergence (creativeemergence.com)

Brian Johnson, en*theos (entheos.com)

Raymond Keene, Keene on Chess (keeneonchess.com)

Mark Levy, Levy Innovation (levyinnovation.com)

Linda Trichter Metcalf, PW Center: Proprioceptive Writing (pwriting.org)

The MogaDao Institute (mogadao.com)

Vanda North, Mind Chi: Change Your Life in 8 Minutes a Day (mindchi.com)

Karen Page (becomingachef.com)

Wendy Palmer, Leadership Embodiment (leadershipembodiment.com)

Robert Peng (robertpeng.com)

Steven Pressfield (stevenpressfield.com)

The Qigong Institute (qigonginstitute.org)

Ken Robinson (sirkenrobinson.com)

Stephen Russell, Barefoot Doctor Presents World Class Consciousness
    (barefootdoctorglobal.com)

SARK (Planetsark.com)

Dale Schusterman, Sign Language of the Soul (signlanguageofthesoul.com)

Burt Swersey, Innovation Junction (burtswersey.blogspot.com)

Robert Tangora (tangorataichi.com)

John Voigt, Art Energy: Qigong for Creativity (art-energy.org)

Win Wenger, PhD, Project Renaissance (winwenger.com)

Michael Winn, Healing Tao USA (healingtaousa.com)

NOTES

These references represent my best attempt to provide appropriate attribution to the sources and inspirations behind the ideas in the text. Any omissions are inadvertent and will be corrected in future editions. Some of the ideas and methods presented in *Creativity On Demand* have been introduced in my previous works. They have, however, been reframed in the context of the revelation that inspired the writing of this book—the idea that mastering the creative mindset and process are ultimately dependent on the ability to master creative energy.

Preface: A Muse of Fire

1. William Shakespeare, *Henry V,* prologue. Available at: shakespeare.mit.edu/henryv/full.html

2. Ken Robinson, *The Element: How Finding Your Passion Changes Everything* (New York: Penguin, 2009), 67.

3. Betty Edwards, *Drawing on the Right Side of the Brain: The Definitive, 4th Edition* (New York: Tarcher/Penguin, 2012), 276.

4. Robert Fritz, *The Path of Least Resistance: Learning to Become the Creative Force in Your Own Life* (New York: Random House, 1989), 11.

5. Steven Pressfield, *The War of Art: Break Through the Blocks and Win Your Inner Creative Battles* (New York: Grand Central Publishing, 2003), 3.

6. Laozi, Stephen Mitchell, trans., *Tao Te Ching* (New York: Harper Perennial, 1992), 8.

Introduction: Ride the Wave

1. Dr. Spencer Johnson, *Who Moved My Cheese?: An Amazing Way to Deal with Change in Your Work and in Your Life* (New York: G. P. Putnam, 1998), 46, 74.

2. Deepak Malhotra, *I Moved Your Cheese: For Those Who Refuse to Live as Mice in Someone Else's Maze* (San Francisco: Berret-Koehler, 2011), 83.

3. IBM Institute for Business Value, "Capitalizing on Complexity: Insights from the Global Chief Executive Officer Study," May 2010. Available at: ibm.com/capitalizingoncomplexity

4. James Clawson, direct communication with the author, November 22, 2013.

5. Ibid.

6. Ibid.

7. Jim Loehr and Tony Schwartz, *The Power of Full Engagement: Managing Energy, Not Time, Is the Key to High Performance and Personal Renewal* (New York: The Free Press, 2005), 197–8.

8. Lynne McTaggart, *The Field: The Quest for the Secret Force of the Universe* (New York: HarperCollins, 2002), xxiii.

9. Rumi, Coleman Barks, trans., *The Essential Rumi, New Expanded Edition* (New York: Harper One, 2004), 138.

10. Deepak Chopra, *The Path to Love: Spiritual Strategies for Healing* (New York: Harmony Books, 1997), 14.

11. Zhuangzi, Raymond B. Blakney, trans., *The Way of Life: Tao Te Ching: The Classic Translation* (New York: Signet, 2001), 95.

12. Carl Sagan, *Cosmos* (New York: Ballantine Books, 1985), 286.

13. Neil deGrasse Tyson, "That's Kinda Cool." Available at: youtube.com/watch?v=UmOThpcCkf4

14. Neil deGrasse Tyson, *Death by Black Hole and Other Cosmic Quandaries* (New York: W. W. Norton, 2007), 222.

15. The Da Vinci Qi Practice, the Ignite and Sustain the Fire of Genius Practice, the Force-to-Power Practice, and others presented here are the result of my experiments with "new combinations of traditional energy-cultivation exercises." The postures and movements in these

practices are adapted from my study with many teachers, but are especially influenced by Ken Cohen, Dean Deng, Robert Peng, Robert Tangora, and The Anonymous Master. I've explored different versions of many of these postures and movements, and the ones presented here are those that I believe will most benefit you. In some cases I developed entirely new movements, such as the Sfumato movement in the Da Vinci Qi Practice and the Love movement in the Force-to-Power Practice.

16. Thanks to Maya Angelou, who noted, "You can't use up creativity. The more you use, the more you have." Quoted in Jeffrey M. Elliot, ed., *Conversations with Maya Angelou* (Jackson, MS: University Press of Mississippi, 1989), x.

17. Eckhart Tolle, *A New Earth: Awakening to Your Life's Purpose* (New York: Penguin, 2008), 302.

Part 1: Mastering Creative Energy

1. Matthew Arnold, *Lectures and Essays in Criticism* (Ann Arbor, MI: University of Michigan Press, 1962), 238.

2. Judith Orloff, *Positive Energy: 10 Extraordinary Prescriptions for Transforming Fatigue, Stress, and Fear into Vibrance, Strength, and Love* (New York: Harmony Books, 2005), 192.

3. Eknath Easwaran, trans., *Bhagavad Gita* (Tomales, CA: Nilgiri Press, 2007), 153.

4. Lou Reed, in an interview with *Kung Fu Magazine*, May 2003.

5. John Keats (letter to his brother and sister-in-law [no. 123], George and Georgiana Keats), Frederick Page, ed., *Letters of John Keats* 1954). Available at: poemhunter.com/quotations/famous. asp?people=john%20keats&p=3

6. Ken Cohen, direct communication with the author, November 17, 2013.

7. Yogananda, the Self-Realization Fellowship. Available at: yogananda-srf.org/HowtoLive/Achieving_True_Success_and_Prosperity.aspx#.Ujs1JLyE76A

8. Martha Graham, in Agnes de Mille, *Martha: The Life and Work of Martha Graham—A Biography* (New York: Random House, 1991), 264.

9. John Voigt, direct communication with the author, June 12, 2013.

10. Osvald Sirén, *The Chinese on the Art of Painting: Texts by the Painter-Critics, from the Han through the Ch'ing Dynasties* (Dover, NY: Dover Publications, 2005), 23.

11. T'ang Hou, in Daniel J. Boorstin, *The Creators: A History of Heroes of the Imagination* (New York: Vintage Books, 1992), chapter 2.

12. Ralph Waldo Emerson, *Essays: Second Series | The Poet* (1844), 12–13. Available at: digireads.com or emersoncentral.com/essays2.htm

13. Carol Rose Brown, direct communication with the author, June 25, 2013.

14. William J. Federer, *George Washington Carver: His Life & Faith in His Own Words* (St. Louis: Amerisearch, Inc., 2002), 72.

15. John Muir, "The National Parks and Forest Reservations," *Sierra Club Bulletin* 1, no. 7 (January 1896): 271–84.

16. Erin M. Shackell and Lionel G. Standing, "Mind Over Matter: Mental Training Increases Physical Strength," *North American Journal of Psychology* 9, no. 1 (2007): 189.

17. This ancient proverb from many cultures was popularized by the book of the same title by Barry Stevens, originally published by The Real People Press in 1970.

18. Friedrich Schiller, in Paul E. Kerry, ed., *Friedrich Schiller: Playwright, Poet, Philosopher, Historian* (Bern, Switzerland: Peter Lang Academic Publishers, 2007), 212.

19. Fran Lebowitz, as quoted on Steven Pinker's Twitter account, March 9, 2013.

20. Swami Beyondananda, direct communication with the author, August 24, 2013.

21. Emily Dickinson, R. W. Franklin, ed., *The Poems of Emily Dickinson* (Boston: Harvard University Press, 1999), 307.

22. Nikola Tesla, "The Problem of Increasing Human Energy," *The Century Magazine,* June 1900, 179.

23. William Blake, *The Marriage of Heaven and Hell* (Oxford, UK: Oxford University Press, 1975), xvii.

24. This practice is based on the work of F. M. Alexander.

25. An earlier version of this practice appeared in *Present Yourself! Captivate Your Audience with Great Presentation Skills* and in *How to Think Like Leonardo da Vinci.*

26. Ken Cohen, direct communication with the author, July 24, 2013.

27. Ibid.

28. Master Chan, quoted by Ken Cohen, direct communication with the author, July 24, 2013.

29. Mette Aadahl et al., "Recent temporal trends in sleep duration, domain-specific sedentary behavior and physical activity. A survey among 25–79-year-old Danish adults," *Scandinavian Journal of Public Health,* June 24, 2013. Available at: sjp.sagepub.com/content/early/20 13/06/21/1403494813493151.abstract

30. Yogananda, the Self-Realization Fellowship.

31. *Science Daily,* April 19, 2012. Available at: sciencedaily.com/ releases/2012/04/120419102317.htm

32. Lorenza S. Colzato et al., "Meditate to Create: The Impact of Focused-Attention and Open-Monitoring Training on Convergent and Divergent Thinking," *Frontiers in Psychology,* 2012, 3 DOI: 10.3389/fpsyg.2012.00116

33. Richard J. Davidson, PhD, direct communication with the author, August 26, 2013.

34. Thich Nhat Hanh, *Peace Is Every Step: The Path of Mindfulness in Everyday Life* (New York: Bantam, 1992), 28.

35. Thomas Jefferson, *The Letters of Thomas Jefferson* (August 19, 1785, to Peter Carr). Available at: avalon.law.yale.edu/18th_century/let31.asp

36. Henry David Thoreau, *A Year in Thoreau's Journal: 1851* (Introduction by H. Daniel Peck) (New York: Penguin Classics, 1993), 165.

37. Julia Cameron, direct communication with the author, April 15, 2013.

38. Robert Peng, direct communication with the author, July 10, 2013.

39. Morihei Ueshiba, John Stevens, trans., *The Art of Peace* (Boston: Shambhala, 2007), 2.

40. Ken Cohen, direct communication with the author, July 29, 2013.

41. C. G. Jung, *The Structure and Dynamics of the Psyche (Collected Works of C. G. Jung, Volume 8)* (Princeton, NJ: Princeton University Press, 1970), 157.

42. William Wordsworth, "Lines Composed a Few Miles Above Tintern Abbey," *The Complete Poetical Works Of William Wordsworth V1* (Whitefish, MT: Kessinger Publishing, 2006), 117.

43. Robert Peng, direct communication with the author, August 26, 2013.

44. Julia Cameron, *The Artist's Way: A Spiritual Path to Higher Creativity* (New York: Tarcher/Putnam, 2002), 3.

45. Jane Barthelemy, direct communication with the author, July 16, 2013.

46. Samuel Taylor Coleridge, T. Ashe, ed., *The Poetical Works of Samuel Taylor Coleridge* ("Fancy in Nubibus") (Whitefish, MT: Kessinger Publishing, 2004), 254.

47. Roger Jahnke, OMD, direct communication with the author, July 17, 2013.

48. Makarand Paranjape, ed., *The Penguin Sri Aurobindo Reader* (New Delhi, India: Penguin India, 1999), 359.

49. Alan Finger, direct communication with the author, July 9, 2013.

50. Ibid.

51. Ibid.

52. Lorie Dechar, direct communication with the author, August 3, 2013.

53. Wendy Palmer, direct communication with the author, July 22, 2013.

54. Ibid.

55. Ibid.

56. Eckhart Tolle, "Eckhart Teachings Facebook Page," March 22, 2012. Available at: facebook.com/Eckharttolle/posts/1015076618262127

57. Arthur Edward Waite, ed., *The Hermetic and Alchemical Writings of Paracelsus* (Whitefish, MT: Kessinger Publishing, 2005), 289.

58. Leonardo da Vinci, *Leonardo on Art and the Artist* (Mineola, NY: Dover, 2002), 150.

59. Michael J. Gelb, *How to Think Like Leonardo Da Vinci: Seven Steps to Genius Every Day* (New York: Delacorte Press, 1998).

60. Dale Schusterman, direct communication with the author, June 7, 2003. (An earlier version of the *Vitruvian Man* exercise appeared in Michael J. Gelb, *Da Vinci Decoded: Discovering the Spiritual Secrets of Leonardo's Seven Principles* [New York: Delacorte Press, 2004], 143–46.)

61. Dean Y. Deng, MD, direct communication with the author, spring 1995.

62. Kaleo and Elise Ching, direct communication with the author, August 29, 2013.

63. Ibid.

64. Dr. Oz, in an interview with Oprah Winfrey, November 1, 2007.

65. Harvard Health Publications, Harvard Medical School, "The health benefits of tai chi," May 2009. Available at: health.harvard. edu/newsletters/Harvard_Womens_Health_Watch/2009/May/ The-health-benefits-of-tai-chi

66. R. Jahnke et al., "A Comprehensive Review of Health Benefits of Qigong and Tai Chi," *American Journal of Health Promotion* 24, no. 6 (July/Aug 2010).

67. Roger Jahnke, direct communication with the author, August 25, 2013.

68. Ibid.

69. William A. Tiller Institute for Psychoenergetic Science. Available at: tiller.org

70. Ibid.

71. William A. Tiller, PhD, "White Paper XXI: Psychoenergetic Science Applied to The Mind-Body Concept," September 2010, 21. Available at: tillerfoundation.com/White%20Paper%20XXI.pdf

72. Ibid.

73. Dickinson Electronic Archives. Available at: archive.emilydickinson.org/ index.html

74. Bruce Lee, John Little, ed., *Striking Thoughts: Bruce Lee's Wisdom for Daily Living* (Boston: Tuttle Publishing, 2000), 90.

75. Elmer E. Green, PhD, et al., "Anomalous Electrostatic Phenomena in Exceptional Subjects," *Subtle Energies* 2, no. 3 (1991): 69–94.

76. Woody Allen confirmed this oft-quoted line in a 2008 interview with Collidor.com, available at: collider.com/entertainment/interviews/

article.asp/aid/8878/tcid/1/pg/2. He also shared the thought in an August 13, 1989, article in William Safire's *New York Times* column, "On Language."

Part 2: Mastering the Creative Mindset

1. John Cleese, Creativity Video Arts Lecture. Viewed at: youtube.com/ watch?v=f9rtmxJrKwc (video no longer available).

2. Material drawn from the website Mindset (mindsetonline.com); from Carol S. Dweck, *Mindset: The New Psychology of Success* (New York: Ballantine Books, 2007); and from direct conversation with the author.

3. "Burns' Heir," *The Simpsons,* 1994.

4. Homer, Alexander Pope, trans., *The Odyssey,* book II, line 312. Available at: gutenberg.org/ebooks/3160

5. "Ira Glass on Storytelling, part 3 of 4." Available at: youtube.com/ watch?v=BI23U7U2aUY (confirmed with Ira Glass).

6. Darya L. Zabelina and Michael D. Robinson, "Don't Be So Hard on Yourself: Self-Compassion Facilitates Creative Originality Among Self-Judgmental Individuals," *Creativity Research Journal* 22, no. 3 (2010): 288–93.

7. Leonardo da Vinci, Irma Richter, ed., *The Notebooks of Leonardo Da Vinci* (Oxford, UK: Oxford University Press, 1982), 249.

8. Kaleo and Elise Ching, direct communication with the author.

9. Ibid.

10. Preliminary versions of this material have been presented in earlier works, including *Lessons From the Art of Juggling* (1994) and *How to Think Like Leonardo da Vinci* (1998).

11. Widely attributed to Johann Wolfgang von Goethe. According to Goethe scholar Raymond Keene, there's no record of this quote in the works of Goethe, but "it is the type of thing he might have said."

12. Sigmund Freud, *Leonardo da Vinci and a Memory of His Childhood* (New York: Norton, 1964), 88.

13. Murray Gell-Mann, direct communication with the author, September 2, 2013.

14. Widely attributed to Ralph Waldo Emerson. Emerson graduated in the middle of his class at Harvard, and as literary wit Forrest Hainline observes, "He no doubt felt his genius underappreciated."

15. Abraham H. Maslow, *Maslow on Management* (New York: John Wiley & Sons, 1998), 13.

16. Darya L. Zabelina and Michael D. Robinson, "Child's Play: Facilitating the Originality of Creative Output by a Priming Manipulation," *Psychology of Aesthetics, Creativity, and the Arts* 4, no. 1 (American Psychological Association, 2010): 57–65.

17. Laura Janecka, "How To Think Like a Kid: Child's play can inspire you," *Psychology Today*, July 01, 2010.

18. Helen Dukas and Banesh Hoffmann, *Albert Einstein, the Human Side: New Glimpses from His Archives* (Princeton, NJ: Princeton University Press, 1981), 83.

19. Matt Groening, interview on the "Simpson Crazy" website. Available at: simpsoncrazy.com/articles/mattgroening

20. Charles Baudelaire, *The Painter of Modern Life and Other Essays (Arts & Letters)* (London: Phaidon Press, 1995), 8.

21. Dean Y. Deng, MD, and Enid Ballin, *Qigong: A Legacy in Chinese Healing* (New Orleans: Qigong International, 1998), 67.

22. Robert McCammon, *Boy's Life* (New York: Simon and Schuster, 1992), 2.

23. Maulána Jalálu-'d-Dín Muhammad Rúmí and Edward Henry Whinfield, trans. (1898), *The Masnavi*, book IV, story II, 278. Available at: thesufi.com/rumi_masnavi.pdf

24. Daniel Ladinsky, *Love Poems from God: Twelve Sacred Voices from the East and West* (New York: Penguin, 2002), 177.

25. Dean Y. Deng, direct communication with the author, spring 1995.

26. Some of this material originally appeared in an article by the author in the magazine *Experience Life,* July/August 2009.

27. W. M. Kelley et al., "The neural funny bone: Dissociating cognitive and affective components of humor," Society for Neuroscience 32nd Annual Meeting, Nov. 2–7, 2002, Orlando, FL.

28. Avner Ziv, "Facilitating effects of humor on creativity," *Journal of Educational Psychology* 68, no. 3 (June 1976): 318–22.

29. Fred Mildler, PhD, direct communication with the author, August 4, 2013.

30. G. K. Chesterton, *Orthodoxy* (San Francisco: Ignatius Press, 1995), chapter VII: The Eternal Revolution.

31. Michelle James, direct communication with the author, July 11, 2013.

32. Thich Nhat Hanh, *Peace Is Every Step: The Path of Mindfulness in Everyday Life* (New York: Bantam, 1992), 6.

33. K. L. Tidd and J. S. Lockard, "Monetary significance of the affiliative smile: A case for reciprocal altruism," *Bulletin of the Psychonomic Society* 11, no. 6 (1978): 6, 344–46.

34. D. G. Walsh and J. Hewitt, "Giving men the come-on: Effect of eye contact and smiling in a bar environment," *Perceptual and Motor Skills* 61 (1985): 873–74.

35. Ernest L. Abel and Michael Kruger, "Smile Intensity in Photographs Predicts Longevity," *Psychological Science* 21 (April 2010): 542–44. First published on February 26, 2010.

36. Kareem J. Johnson et al., "Smile to see the forest: Facially expressed positive emotions broaden cognition," *Cognition & Emotion* 24, no. 2 (2010): 299–321.

37. Elizabeth Gilbert, *Eat, Pray, Love: One Woman's Search for Everything Across Italy, India and Indonesia* (New York: Penguin, 2007), 231.

38. Michael Winn, direct communication with the author, June 11, 2013.

39. Percy B. Shelley, *Prometheus Unbound: A Lyrical Drama in Four Acts* (London: Black Box Press, 2007), 40.

40. Mingtong Gu, direct communication with the author, December 24, 2013.

41. Also translated as, "He who is fixed to a star." Da Vinci, Richter, ed., 249.

42. Friedrich Nietzsche, *The Twilight of the Idols and The Anti-Christ: or How to Philosophize with a Hammer,* "Maxims and Arrows, #12" (London: Penguin Classics, 1990), 33.

43. C. G. Jung, *Synchronicity: An Acausal Connecting Principle* (from Vol. 8 of the *Collected Works of C. G. Jung*) (Princeton, NJ: Princeton University Press, 2010), 20.

44. Often falsely attributed to the Buddha, this proverb is found in different forms in many different traditions.

45. Mingtong Gu, direct communication with the author, December 24, 2013.

46. Ibid.

47. Ibid.

48. Ibid.

49. Hank Aaron, *I Had a Hammer: The Hank Aaron Story* (New York: HarperCollins, 2009), chapter 8.

50. Da Vinci, Richter, ed., 323.

51. Dr. Shirley Ann Jackson, president of Rensselaer Polytechnic Institute, "Expediting Serendipity: Building an Innovation Ecosystem," a speech to the Detroit Economic Club, October 8, 2009.

52. Wislawa Szymborska, "The Poet and the World" (1996) Nobel lecture. Available at: nobelprize.org/nobel_prizes/literature/laureates/1996/szymborska-lecture.html

53. Jeff Sandefer, "The One Key Trait for Successful Entrepreneurs: A Tolerance for Ambiguity," Forbes.com, May 17, 2012. Available at: forbes.com/sites/acton/2012/05/17/the-one-key-trait-for-successful-entrepreneurs-a-tolerance-for-ambiguity/

54. Theodor Adorno et al., *The Authoritarian Personality* (New York: W. W. Norton Company, 1993).

55. Vanda North, direct communication with the author.

56. Ibid.

57. Ibid.

58. IBM Institute for Business Value, "Capitalizing on Complexity: Insights from the Global Chief Executive Officer Study," May 2010. Available at: ibm.com/capitalizingoncomplexity

59. This meditation is adapted from the Yi Quan qigong system as taught by Ken Cohen.

60. Rumi, Coleman Barks, trans., *The Essential Rumi* (New York: HarperCollins, 1996), 40.

61. Aristotle, *Nicomachean Ethics* (Indianapolis, IN: Hackett Publishing Co., 1999).

62. "The Chutzpah Principle of Intelligence" was introduced in my 1995 Harmony Books release *Thinking for a Change: Discovering the Power to Create, Communicate, and Lead.*

63. Arthur Ransome, *Oscar Wilde: A Critical Study* (New York: Mitchell Kennerley, 1912), 64. Available at: openlibrary.org/books/ OL14032796M/Oscar_Wilde. For an in-depth consideration of the legitimacy of this quote, please visit: oscarwildeinamerica.org/ quotations/nothing-to-declare.html

64. Sir Jeremy Irons, interview with the Academy of Achievement, October 27, 2000. Available at: achievement.org/autodoc/page/iro0int-1

65. Maseena Ziegler, "Why Chutzpah Is the New Charisma - And How To Use It To Get What You Want," ForbesWoman, 5/18/2012. Available at: forbes.com/sites/crossingborders/2012/05/18/why-chutzpah-is-the-new-charisma-and-how-to-use-it-to-get-what-you-want/

66. Amy Elizabeth Fox, direct communication with the author, August 20, 2013.

67. Sir Richard Branson. Available at: virgin.com/richard-branson/ say-yes-then-learn-how-to-do-it-later

68. Rollo May, *Man's Search for Himself* (New York: W. W. Norton, 1953), 169.

69. Frank Dyer and Thomas Martin, *Edison: His Life and Inventions,* chapter XXVIII. Available at: gutenberg.org/ebooks/820

70. Carl Sagan, *Broca's Brain: Reflections on the Romance of Science* (New York: Ballantine Books, 1986), 75.

71. Rene' Vallery-Radot, *The Life of Pasteur* (Forgotten Books, 2012), 79. From a lecture Pasteur gave at the University of Lille, France, on December 7, 1874. (The original French: *Dans les champs de l'observation le hasard ne favorise que les esprits prepares.*) Available at: forgottenbooks.org/books/The_Life_of_Pasteur_1000588560

72. George Bancroft, *The Necessity, the Reality, and the Promise of the Progress of the Human Race* (Whitefish, MT: Kessinger Publishing, 2010), 13. Oration delivered before the New York Historical Society, November 20, 1854.

73. Plato, *Symposium* (New York: Penguin Classics, 1999).

74. I've written about comparative appreciation in earlier works, including *How to Think Like Leonardo da Vinci, Wine Drinking for Inspired Thinking,* and in an article for the magazine *Experience Life* in April 2010.

75. Jacob Bronowski, *Science and Human Values* (London: Faber and Faber, 2011), 9.

76. Murray Gell-Mann, direct communication with the author, September 3, 2013.

77. R. A. Atchley et al., "Creativity in the Wild: Improving Creative Reasoning through Immersion in Natural Settings" (2012), PLoS ONE 7(12): e51474. doi:10.1371/journal.pone.0051474

78. John Muir, *Our National Parks* (New York: Houghton Mifflin Company, 1901), 56.

79. Homer, Samuel Butler, trans., *The Odyssey* (Digireads: 2009), book III, 32.

80. H. Anna Suh, *Van Gogh's Letters: The Mind of the Artist in Painting, Drawings, and Words, 1875–1890* (New York: Black Dog & Leventhal Publishers, 2010), 223.

81. Jolande Székács Jacobi, *The Psychology of Jung: An Introduction with Illustrations* (New Haven, CT: Yale University Press, 1973), 25.

82. G. K. Chesterton, in Jane Yolen, "The Sleep of Trees," *Tales of Wonder* (New York: Schocken Books, 1987), 33.

83. Johannes Brahms, in Profiles of Great Classical Composers: 52composers.com/brahms.html

84. Eliza Farnham, *Woman and Her Era,* vol. 1 (New York: A. J. Davis, 1864), 122.

85. Lee Siegel, "Where Have All the Muses Gone?", *Wall Street Journal,* May 16, 2009. Available at: online.wsj.com/article/SB124242927020125473.html

86. Morihei Ueshiba, John Stevens, trans., *The Heart of Aikido: The Philosophy of Takemusu Aiki* (New York: Kodansha USA, 2013), 54.

87. Bill Douglas, direct communication with the author, July 18, 2013.

88. Ibid.

89. Ibid.

90. Carol Dweck, "Developing Growth Mindsets: How Praise Can Harm, and How to Use it Well," keynote speech at the Scottish Learning Festival, September 23, 2009. Available at: educationscotland.gov.uk/video/c/video_tcm4565678.asp

91. Ken Robinson, *The Element: How Finding Your Passion Changes Everything* (New York: Penguin, 2009), 24.

92. Adriaan D. De Groot, *Thought and Choice in Chess* (Amsterdam: Amsterdam University Press, 2008).

93. Raymond Keene, direct communication with the author, December 1, 2013.

94. K. Anders Ericsson, *The Road to Excellence: The Acquisition of Expert Performance in the Arts and Sciences, Sports, and Games* (Abingdon, UK: Lawrence Erlbaum Associates, 1996). Note: de Groot and Ericsson were cited in *More Balls Than Hands*.

Part 3: Mastering the Creative Process

1. Often attributed to Sir Francis Bacon, this quote is actually a translation of his words into contemporary language. He wrote: "There is something insane and self-contradictory in supposing that things that have never yet been done can be done except by means never tried."

2. Thanks to Dr. Edward de Bono for inspiring this idea.

3. Abraham Maslow, *The Psychology of Science: A Reconnaissance* (1966) chapter 2, 15 (available as an ebook from Maurice Bassett Publishing: abrahammaslow.com/books.html).

4. An earlier version of the five phases appeared in *Thinking for a Change*.

5. G. K. Chesterton, *The Scandal of Father Brown* (W. Valley City, UT: Waking Lion Press, 2006), 134.

6. Simon Turnbull, "Olympics: Four decades later we're all still doing the Fosbury Flop," *The Independent*, July 27, 2008. Available at: independent.co.uk/sport/olympics/olympics-four-decades-later-were-all-still-doing-the-fosbury-flop-878314.html

7. Ian Frazier, "Form and Fungus," *The New Yorker*, May 20, 2013.

8. Ibid.

9. Quote widely attributed to William James.

10. Sir Joshua Reynolds, *The Works of Sir Joshua Reynolds, 4th edition: Discourses on Art,* discourse no. 2, vol. 1 (London: T. Cadell and W. Davies Publishers, 1809), 28.

11. Thanks to Win Wenger, PhD, for emphasizing the importance of writing down the problem.

12. J. Krishnamurti, *Life Ahead: On Learning and the Search for Meaning* (Novato, CA: New World Library, 2005), 120.

13. William James, *Psychology: The Briefer Course* (New York: Harper and Row, 1961), 195.

14. Robert Ornstein, PhD, *The Evolution of Consciousness: The Origins of the Way We Think* (New York: Simon & Schuster, 1992), 246.

15. Linus Pauling, quoted by Francis Crick in his presentation "The Impact of Linus Pauling on Molecular Biology," Oregon State University, 1995.

16. Thomas Edison, in Frank Dyer and Lewis Martin, *Edison: His Life and Inventions,* xxiv. Available at: gutenberg.org/ebooks/820

17. Da Vinci, Richter, ed., 178.

18. Thomas Fensch, ed., *Conversations with John Steinbeck* (Jackson, MS: University Press of Mississippi, 1988), 43.

19. Alfred Nobel, quoted in Linus Pauling's Acceptance Speech, on the occasion of the award of the Nobel Peace Prize in Oslo, Norway, December 10, 1963. Available at: nobelprize.org/nobel_prizes/peace/laureates/1962/pauling-acceptance_en.html

20. This quote is sometimes attributed to advertising pioneer Charles Brower, who used it in an article in *Advertising Age* magazine. And it is also believed by many to have originated with the Roman poet Ovid (43 BCE–18 CE). Ovid is best known as the author of *The Metamorphoses* and as an important source of classical mythology. This quote is widely attributed to him, but since no source is available we don't know if it's apocryphal.

21. Friedrich Schiller, in Anna Herbert, *The Pedagogy of Creativity* (London: Routledge, 2010), 43.

22. Stephen Russell, direct communication with the author, April 14, 2013.

23. Ibid.

24. Gertrude Stein, *Everybody's Autobiography* (Chicago: Exact Change Press, 2004), chapter 2.

25. Giorgio Vasari, *The Lives of the Artists* (Oxford, UK: Oxford University Press, 2008), 290.

26. Da Vinci, Richter, ed., 188.

27. Henri Poincaré, in Rollo May, *The Courage to Create* (New York: W. W. Norton & Company, 1994), 65.

28. Steven Pressfield, *The War of Art: Break Through the Blocks and Win Your Inner Creative Battles* (New York: Grand Central Publishing, 2003), 125–6.

29. Judy Collins, in Alex J. Packer, *Wise Highs: How to Thrill, Chill, and Get Away from It All Without Alcohol or Other Drugs* (Minneapolis: Free Spirit Publishing, 2006), 213.

30. John Cleese, Creativity Video Arts Lecture. Accessed at: youtube.com/watch?v=f9rtmxJrKwc

31. Conrad Hilton, *Be My Guest* (New York: Fireside, 1994), 196.

32. Jon Miller, direct communication with the author, July 1, 2013.

33. E. J. Applewhite, *Cosmic Fishing: An Account of Writing Synergetics with Buckminster Fuller* (New York: Macmillan Company, 1977).

34. Emily Dickinson, Thomas H. Johnson, ed., *The Complete Poems of Emily Dickinson* (New York: Back Bay Books, 1976), 327.

35. Edward de Bono, *Lateral Thinking: Creativity Step by Step* (New York: Harper & Row, 1970), 159.

36. Niccolò Machiavelli, *The Prince* (New York: Bantam Classics, 1984), chapter 15.

37. Widely attributed to Herman Kahn.

38. Tina Fey, *Bossypants* (New York: Reagan Little Brown, 2013), 203.

39. Weston H. Agor, *The Logic of Intuitive Decision Making: A Research-Based Approach for Top Management* (New York: Quorum Books, 1986), xiv.

40. LeBron James on *Good Morning America*, August 12, 2013.

41. Kroc's story is number seven on Oprah's timeline of "Great Moments in Intuition." Available at: oprah.com/spirit/A-History-of-Intuition-Intuition-Timeline/7

42. Eugene Gendlin, *Focusing* (New York: Bantam Books, 1982).

43. Jim Alexander, direct communication with the author, December 7, 2013.

44. Ibid.

45. Ibid.

46. Nolan Bushnell, entrepreneur, featured in *Newsweek*'s "50 Men Who Changed America." Bushnell, on his website, nolanbushnell.com, states that this is his favorite maxim.

47. Richard K. Wagner, "Smart People Doing Dumb Things: The Case of Managerial Incompetence," in Robert Sternberg, ed., *Why Smart People Can Be So Stupid* (Princeton, NJ: Yale University Press, 2003), 42–63.

48. Robert Sternberg, *Successful Intelligence: How Practical and Creative Intelligence Determine Success in Life* (New York: Plume, 1997).

49. Henry David Thoreau, *Walden (Or Life in the Woods)* (Radford, Virginia: Wilder Publications, 2008), 198.

50. Bennett Goodspeed, direct communication with the author, January 1982.

51. A. N. Whitehead, *Dialogues of Alfred North Whitehead* (Boston: Little Brown, 1954), 98.

52. "High level of practical intelligence a factor in entrepreneurial success," *Science Daily* (October 30, 2010) interview with J. Robert Baum. Available at: sciencedaily.com/releases/2010/10/101027153543.htm

53. Paul Israel, *Edison: A Life of Invention* (New York: John Wiley & Sons, 2000), 119–41.

54. The SMART EDISON acronym was introduced in Michael J. Gelb and Sarah Miller Caldicott, *Innovate Like Edison: The Success System of America's Greatest Inventor* (New York: Dutton, 2007), 50–1.

55. Thomas Edison, in *The Edison & Ford Quote Book* (Fort Myers, FL: Edison and Ford Winter Estates, 2004), 24. Available at: edisonfordwinterestates.org/store/Edison-Ford-Quote-Book.html

56. Edward de Bono, *Six Thinking Hats* (New York: Little Brown & Co., 1985).

57. William Blake, *The Marriage of Heaven and Hell* (Oxford, UK: Oxford University Press, 1975), xvii.

58. Al Huang, direct communication with the author, June 10, 2013.

59. Bill Gallen, direct communication with the author, May 24, 2013.

60. Ibid.

61. Ibid.

62. I've championed Mind Mapping in many previous works.

63. Madhu Jayawant, PhD, direct communication with the author, March 1992.

64. Daniel Kahneman, in Michael Schrage, "Daniel Kahneman: The Thought Leader Interview," *Strategy + Business* no. 33 (winter 2003). Available at: strategy-business.com/article/03409?pg=all

65. Kahneman, *Thinking, Fast and Slow* (New York: Farrar, Straus and Giroux, 2011).

66. Kahneman, in Michael Schrage, "Daniel Kahneman: The Thought Leader Interview."

67. Attributed to George Bernard Shaw, but no source is available. It is, however, the kind of thing that Shaw might have said.

68. Blake, *The Marriage of Heaven and Hell*, xxii.

69. William Wordsworth, Letter to his Wife (April 29, 1812). Available at: en.wikiquote.org/wiki/William_Wordsworth

70. Mary Oliver, in Maria Shriver, "Maria Shriver Interviews the Famously Private Poet Mary Oliver," Oprah.com, March 9, 2011. Available at: oprah.com/entertainment/ Maria-Shriver-Interviews-Poet-Mary-Oliver/2

71. John Locke, "A Letter from Mr. Locke to Mr. Samuel Bold. - [May 16, 1699]," *The Works of John Locke in Nine Volumes* (London: Rivington, 1824), 12th ed., vol. 9.

72. Linda Trichter Metcalf, direct communication with the author, August 27, 2013.

73. Brian Johnson, direct communication with the author, August 27, 2013.

74. Jonah Lehrer, "Groupthink: The Brainstorming Myth," *The New Yorker*, January 30, 2012.

75. Mata Amritanandamayi (Amma). Available at: http://www.quoteswave.com/text-quotes/451956

76. Blake, *The Marriage of Heaven and Hell,* xxii.

77. Quote available at: New World Encyclopedia, newworldencyclopedia.org/entry/Johannes_Brahms; and Profiles of Great Classical Composers, 52composers.com/brahms.html

78. Johnny Cash, interview with the Academy of Achievement, June 25, 1993. Available at: achievement.org/autodoc/page/cas0int-3

79. Nikola Tesla, *My Inventions: The Autobiography of Nikola Tesla* (New York: Soho Books, 1983), 64.

80. Ibid., 42.

Part 4: Mastering Creative Energy, Mindset, and Process: Moving from Force to Power

1. David Hawkins, MD, PhD, *Power vs. Force: The Hidden Determinants of Human Behavior* (Carlsbad, CA: Hay House, 2002), 285.

2. Rollo May, *The Courage to Create,* 13.

3. William Wordsworth, *The Collected Poems of William Wordsworth* (Hertfordshire, UK: Wordsworth Poetry Library, 1998), vol. 1.

4. A number of the movements in the Force-to-Power Practice are adapted from the teachings of The Anonymous Master.

5. Hawkins, *Power vs. Force,* 195.

Afterword: Who Moved My Qi?

1. Kevin Ashton, "That 'Internet of Things' Thing," *RFID Journal,* June 22, 2009. Available at: rfidjournal.com/articles/view?4986

2. Quote available at J. Krishnamurti Online: jkrishnamurti.org/krishnamurti-teachings/view-daily-quote/20090711.php?t=Life

3. Ibid.

4. Quote available at J. Krishnamurti Online: jkrishnamurti.org/krishnamurti-teachings/view-daily-quote/20110605.php

ABOUT THE AUTHOR

Michael J. Gelb is the world's leading authority on applying genius thinking to personal and organizational development. He is a pioneer in the fields of creative thinking, mind-body integration, and innovative leadership. For more than thirty-five years, he has guided organizations to develop cultures that promote creativity and innovation. His clients include Hunter Roberts Construction Group, Genentech, the Institute for Management Studies, Microsoft, and the Young Presidents' Organization. His work has been featured on NPR, PBS, and *Good Morning America,* and in the *New York Times, Washington Post,* and *USA Today,* as well as in *Forbes, INC,* and *Training* magazines.

He is the author of fourteen books, including the international best seller *How to Think Like Leonardo da Vinci.* In 1999, he won The Brain Trust Charity's "Brain of the Year" award; other honorees include Stephen Hawking, Bill Gates, Garry Kasparov, and Gene Rodenberry. In 2003, Michael was awarded a Batten Fellowship by the University of Virginia's Darden Graduate School of Business. He codirects the acclaimed Leading Innovation Seminar at Darden with Professor James Clawson.

A former professional juggler who once performed with The Rolling Stones, Michael is also a fourth-degree black belt in aikido, a certified teacher of the Alexander Technique, a certified teacher of Chinese energy arts, and a teaching member of the Qigong Institute. He is renowned for the scintillating creative energy he brings to all his programs, including public offerings at the Omega Institute and the Esalen Institute.

ABOUT SOUNDS TRUE

Sounds True is a multimedia publisher whose mission is to inspire and support personal transformation and spiritual awakening. Founded in 1985 and located in Boulder, Colorado, we work with many of the leading spiritual teachers, thinkers, healers, and visionary artists of our time. We strive with every title to preserve the essential "living wisdom" of the author or artist. It is our goal to create products that not only provide information to a reader or listener, but that also embody the quality of a wisdom transmission.

For those seeking genuine transformation, Sounds True is your trusted partner. At SoundsTrue.com you will find a wealth of free resources to support your journey, including exclusive weekly audio interviews, free downloads, interactive learning tools, and other special savings on all our titles.

To learn more, please visit SoundsTrue.com/bonus/free_gifts or call us toll free at 800-333-9185.

SOUNDS TRUE
many voices, one journey